THE NEW DOCTOR NOW DIET PLAN

10 Week Meal Plan Offering Simple, Effective Nutrition Solutions to Help You Shed Pounds, Revitalize Your Lifestyle, and Feel Your Best

Lenora Weatherford

TABLE OF CONTENTS

CHAPTER 1: UNDERSTANDING THE FOUNDATIONS OF HEALTHY EATING

1.1 THE SCIENCE BEHIND METABOLISM AND WEIGHT LOSS

Imagine your body as a finely-tuned engine. Just like a car needs fuel to run, your body needs food. The process by which your body converts what you eat and drink into energy is called metabolism. It's a complex biochemical process where calories in food and beverages are combined with oxygen to release the energy your body needs to function. Sometimes, understanding this can make all the difference in how we approach weight loss and health.

Metabolism often gets the blame when people talk about weight loss challenges. It's common to hear someone frustrated with dieting say, "I just have a slow metabolism." However, what many don't realize is that the rate of metabolism is closely tied to our physical activity, muscle mass, and overall body composition, not just an inherent speed at which our body processes calories.

Let's delve deeper. Metabolism actually comprises several components, primarily basal metabolic rate (BMR), which accounts for about 70% of the calories you burn each day. BMR is the amount of energy (calories) your body needs to perform basic life-sustaining functions like breathing, circulation, cell production, nutrient processing, and temperature regulation. Factors that influence your BMR include age, sex, genetics, body size, and muscle mass. Typically, the larger or more muscular you are, the higher your BMR. This is why resistance training that builds lean muscle is often key in effectively managing your weight – it literally helps you burn more calories, even when you're at rest.

Thermogenesis is another aspect of your metabolism, involving the production of heat in your body. It's the energy used during digestion to turn food into fuel your body can use, commonly referred to as the thermic effect of food (TEF). For instance, protein has a higher thermic effect compared to fats or carbohydrates. This means your body uses more energy to digest protein than it does for other types of foods, which is partly why high-protein diets can boost metabolism and speed up weight loss. Your activity level forms the final piece of the metabolic puzzle. Physical activity and exercise not only increase the calories you burn during the activity but also boost your overall metabolic rate for hours afterwards. This is often termed as the 'afterburn effect' or post-exercise oxygen consumption (EPOC). Engaging regularly in high-intensity exercises like sprints, circuit training, or even brisk walking can increase your EPOC, thus enhancing your ability to lose weight more effectively.

Now, turning this understanding into weight loss success requires a holistic approach. Firstly, it's crucial to debunk a common myth: dramatically lowering calorie intake can boost weight loss. While it sounds logical, excessively cutting calories can cause your metabolism to slow down, a survival mechanism from our ancestors' days when food was scarce. This adaptation can lead to a frustrating plateau in your weight loss journey.

Instead, focus on creating a balanced diet with a mix of macronutrients—proteins, fats, and carbohydrates—designed to meet your body's needs without excessive calorie restrictions. Remember, proteins are particularly beneficial because of their high TEF. Incorporate healthy fats, which although calorically dense, provide longer satiety, helping reduce overall calorie intake. As for carbs, opting for whole grains provide sustained energy without the spikes in blood sugar that lead to fat storage.

Moreover, it's essential not to ignore the other factors enhancing metabolism such as hydration, adequate sleep, and managing stress. Each plays a significant role in how effectively your body operates. Chronic stress, for instance, can lead to an increase in cortisol, a hormone that not only encourages fat storage, particularly around the mid-section, but can also slow down your metabolism. Similarly, lack of adequate sleep can interrupt the regulation of hormones like insulin, leading to increased hunger and weight gain.

The key is consistency and making lifestyle changes you can maintain. Frequent, smaller meals can keep your metabolism more consistently engaged throughout the day. Hydrating well assists in maintaining optimal metabolic function and aids in digestion and nutrient absorption. Ensuring you get enough sleep and managing stress through techniques like mindfulness or yoga can have cumulative positive effects on your metabolic rate.

In summary, unlocking the science behind metabolism and weight loss offers a clear path forward. It challenges the conventional wisdom of simply cutting calories drastically and highlights the benefits of a well-rounded approach that includes diet, exercise, and other lifestyle factors. By tuning into your body's needs and responding with thoughtful, well-informed choices, achieving your health goals becomes not just a possibility, but a sustainable reality. Remember, the goal of "The New Doctor Now Diet Plan" is not just to lose weight, but to understand the underlying principles that will help you maintain your health over a lifetime.

1.2 THE ROLE OF MACRONUTRIENTS: PROTEIN, CARBS, AND FATS

In our journey toward a healthier self, understanding the role of macronutrients— proteins, carbohydrates, and fats—in our diet is a bit like learning to balance a seesaw. Too much or too little on one end, and you'll find yourself stuck in the mud or flung unexpectedly into the air. Let's explore how these essential nutrients work together to keep you balanced, energized, and on a path to sustained weight loss and wellness.

Starting with **proteins**, consider them the building blocks of life. Every cell in your body contains protein, which means it's crucial for not just muscle repair and growth but also for the creation and maintenance of bones, hormones, enzymes, and skin. Imagine a busy construction site; that's what protein looks like in your body, constantly building and repairing.

The thermic effect of protein is also noteworthy. Unlike fats or carbohydrates, protein uses a significant chunk of the calories it delivers just to digest and metabolize. This thermogenic property makes protein extremely valuable for weight loss. Eating protein-rich foods can also make you feel fuller longer, hence reducing the overall caloric intake. Foods like chicken, fish, tofu, legumes, eggs, and dairy products are excellent sources of high-quality protein.

Next, let's talk about **carbohydrates**, often unfairly demonized in diet culture. It's essential to understand that not all carbs are created equal. Carbohydrates are your body's main fuel source, broken down into glucose, which your cells use for energy. Now, imagine your body as a car again — carbs are the gasoline that keeps you running.

However, the type of carbohydrate matters immensely. Simple carbs, like those in sugary drinks, desserts, and processed foods, can spike blood sugar levels leading to increased fat storage if the energy provided isn't used. Complex carbs, found in whole grains, vegetables, and fruits, digest slower and provide a steadier source of energy without the spikes and crashes associated with simple sugars. They also offer dietary fiber, which aids digestive health and also helps to manage cholesterol.

Last but equally essential are **fats**, which have long suffered from a lot of bad press. However, healthy fats are crucial to brain health, energy, absorption of certain vitamins, and to keep your body running smoothly. Think of fats as a reserve of energy: They provide sustenance when you're running low, much like a backup generator.

There are several types of fats, but the focus should be on unsaturated fats. These can be found in olive oil, avocados, nuts, and fish, and they help fight inflammation, provide cell structure, and make food taste better without the detrimental effects on heart health associated with saturated and trans fats.

What many people don't realize is that a healthy diet needs a thoughtful balance of these macronutrients. Modern dietary guidelines suggest varying one's macronutrient intake, typically recommending that around 45-65% of your daily calories come from carbohydrates, 20-35% from fats, and 10-35% from proteins. This balance can, of course, be adjusted depending on personal health goals, activity levels, and medical advice. For instance, someone looking to lose weight and build muscle might increase their protein intake relative to carbs and fats, while someone preparing for a marathon might increase their carb intake for added energy. It's like mixing paint— different goals require different combinations of primary colors, or in this case, macronutrients.

Understanding how to balance these macronutrients in your diet isn't just about counting calories or following rigid rules. It's about listening to your body and responding to its needs with a varied, balanced diet that fuels both your physical activities and your overall health. Regular meals composed of balanced macronutrients can help regulate blood sugar levels, curb cravings, and avoid the common pitfalls of both overeating and overly restrictive dieting.

As you continue your path forward, consider macronutrients your friends and allies in health. Each has its unique role and function, contributing to a well-rounded diet. Keeping this balance isn't merely about looking good—it's about fueling your body and mind for the challenges ahead and ensuring that you're building a foundation of health that will last a lifetime. So, next time you plan your meal, think of the construction site, the car fueling up, and the backup generator—all parts of the complex but beautiful system that is your body's metabolism. Here's to finding the perfect balance on your plate and in your life.

1.3 HYDRATION AND ITS IMPACT ON WEIGHT AND ENERGY

Imagine a river flowing effortlessly through a lush landscape, nourishing everything in its path. This image captures the essence of the role that water plays within our bodies—silently, effectively, a life force central to our very existence. On the quest for optimal health, weight management, and elevated energy, water is not merely a facet; it is a foundation.

Hydration does more than quench thirst; it influences how every system in our body functions, including the mechanisms that govern weight loss and energy levels. Just as a river supports an entire ecosystem, water supports your metabolism, maintaining the fluid balance necessary for processes such as nutrient transportation, body temperature regulation, and digestion.

Let's examine the understated impact water has on metabolic rates and weight. The process of thermogenesis, where our body metabolizes food into energy, requires adequate hydration to function optimally. Studies indicate that drinking water can temporarily boost metabolism by urging the body to expend more calories. An interesting phenomenon occurs when we drink cold water. Our body expends additional energy to heat the water to body temperature, enhancing this metabolic effect. Furthermore, water is a natural appetite suppressant. Often, we confuse thirst for hunger, leading to overeating. Regular water intake can help maintain the balance by ensuring that we only eat when truly hungry.

On the question of energy, dehydration is a notorious culprit for fatigue. Our bloodstream maintains a certain water level to function effectively; a drop in this level means a thicker, more viscous blood consistency, making it more difficult for your heart to circulate oxygen and essential nutrients. The result? A depleted energy state, where even simple tasks feel taxing.

Moreover, adequate water intake supports the liver and kidneys, organs critical to waste elimination and toxin removal. If dehydrated, the efficiency of these processes diminishes and can contribute to weight gain or prevent weight loss, as your body starts retaining more fluid to compensate for losses. It's a paradox that by retaining water, the body actually conserves water, leading to swelling and a few extra pounds on the scales.

However, despite these critical roles, hydration is often the overlooked hero. Many of us walk through our days in a state of low-grade dehydration, acclimating to a baseline that's far from optimal. Symptoms like ongoing headaches, dry skin, and constipation are commonly accepted as minor annoyances when they are actually calls for hydration.

Let's shift our focus from how much to drink, to how to recognize when you've had enough, a constancy rather than a quota. The old adage of 'eight glasses a day' is a good standard, but hydration needs can vary based on factors like age, climate, activity level, and overall health. An alternative method is to observe the color of your urine; pale and clear indicates good hydration, while a dark color suggests a need to drink more water.

Hydration extends beyond just drinking water. Many fruits and vegetables are hydrating; cucumbers, celery, oranges, and melons, for example, have high water content and provide a dual role of hydrating and nourishing your body with essential nutrients and fiber. On the flip side, excessive amounts of caffeinated or alcoholic beverages promote dehydration, despite their fluid content, due to their diuretic effects. To integrate effective hydration into your daily routine, start by linking water intake with established habits. Drink a glass of water upon waking, one with each meal, and when you go to bed. Include hydration-rich foods in your diet and keep a reusable water bottle handy throughout your day. Embrace herbal teas and flavored waters if plain water doesn't appeal to you; these can make hydration more enjoyable without the added sugars found in many commercial beverages.

Understanding and managing hydration can transform your approach to health and weight management. Just as a river shapes the landscape through which it flows, water shapes our health by infiltrating every cell and system in our bodies. It's a simple yet profound lever to enhance your metabolic efficiency, energy levels, and overall well-being. In your journey toward better health, give water the priority it deserves, and like the river, let its persistent flow carve out a path to a healthier you.

1.4 THE IMPORTANCE OF MICRONUTRIENTS: VITAMINS AND MINERALS

Imagine walking into a garden brimming with vibrant life. Each plant, no matter how small or towering, plays a unique role in the ecosystem—an invisible harmony that sustains the environment. Now, picture your body as that garden. Just as the garden relies on the right mix of sunlight, water, and nutrients to thrive, your body depends on a complex balance of vitamins and minerals to function optimally. These micronutrients, though needed in small amounts, are pivotal in driving everything from energy production to immune function. While macronutrients like carbohydrates, proteins, and fats often take center stage in discussions of nutrition, it's the unsung heroes—micronutrients—that work behind the scenes, ensuring that the foundation of your health remains strong.

At their core, vitamins and minerals are catalysts. They don't provide energy directly, but they enable the biochemical reactions that power every cell in your body. Without them, it's like trying to run a high-performance machine without oil: eventually, systems will begin to falter. While deficiencies are less common in modern diets, they do exist, and they can be detrimental to both short-term vitality and long-term health. But just as with anything, too much of a good thing can also tip the scales, leading to imbalances or toxicities that can have serious consequences. Understanding the delicate role these micronutrients play allows us to better grasp why they are essential to the very foundation of healthy eating.

The Essentiality of Vitamins

Vitamins, those tiny compounds we've all heard about since childhood, are the organic molecules our bodies either can't produce at all, or can't produce in sufficient quantities. They must come from the food we eat. Divided into two broad categories— fat-soluble (like vitamins A, D, E, and K) and water-soluble (such as the B-complex vitamins and vitamin C)—they influence an array of bodily processes that are far more intricate than the simplified messages we often receive from food packaging and advertisements.

Take vitamin A, for instance. More than just the "eye vitamin," it plays a key role in maintaining skin health, supporting the immune system, and even regulating cell growth. Vitamin D, often called the "sunshine vitamin" because of how it's synthesized through exposure to sunlight, influences bone health, helping the body absorb calcium. Yet, its role doesn't stop there. Research increasingly suggests vitamin D plays a part in mental health, with correlations being drawn between deficiencies and mood disorders such as depression. These connections underscore the often subtle, yet profound, impact that micronutrient imbalances can have on overall well-being. Water-soluble vitamins, on the other hand, are not stored in the body and thus need to be replenished more frequently. The B vitamins, particularly, are involved in energy metabolism—ensuring the food you eat is effectively turned into energy your body can use. Consider vitamin B12, one of the most discussed of the B-complex group. Essential for red blood cell formation and neurological function, B12 is unique in that it is primarily found in animal products, making it a potential concern for vegans and vegetarians. A deficiency in B12 can creep up slowly, leading to symptoms like fatigue, memory problems, and even nerve damage if left unchecked. It's a small but crucial part of the nutrition puzzle, illustrating how even a single vitamin, when lacking, can send ripples through various systems of the body.

Vitamin C, perhaps the most famous of all, is known for its role in supporting immune function, but it's also a powerful antioxidant. It helps in wound healing, the maintenance of cartilage, bones, and teeth, and plays a role in collagen production, which is vital for healthy skin and connective tissues. Its ability to combat free radicals—the unstable molecules that can cause oxidative stress—makes it a key player in reducing the risk of chronic diseases, from heart disease to certain cancers.

The Unsung Role of Minerals

While vitamins often steal the spotlight, minerals are equally crucial to our well-being. These inorganic elements, found in soil and water, are absorbed by plants and animals, making their way into our diets through the foods we eat. They are involved in everything from maintaining fluid balance to building strong bones and teeth.

Take calcium, a mineral often associated with dairy products and bone health. While it's true that calcium is vital for strong bones, it's also involved in muscle function, nerve transmission, and the release of hormones. However, calcium doesn't work alone. It has a symbiotic relationship with other micronutrients, particularly vitamin D, which helps the body absorb calcium more effectively. Without enough vitamin D, even a calcium-rich diet might not yield the benefits we expect. Iron is another mineral with far-reaching effects. Critical for the production of hemoglobin, the protein in red blood cells that carries oxygen throughout the body, iron ensures that your muscles, tissues, and organs receive the oxygen they need to function properly. A deficiency in iron can lead to anemia, a condition characterized by fatigue, weakness, and shortness of breath. Women, in particular, are more susceptible to iron deficiency due to menstrual blood loss, and it's important to recognize how this small mineral plays such a large role in day-to-day energy levels.

Then there's magnesium, a powerhouse mineral involved in more than 300 biochemical reactions in the body. From muscle relaxation to energy production, magnesium helps regulate blood pressure, supports immune function, and keeps the heartbeat steady. Interestingly, it's also been linked to better sleep and reduced symptoms of anxiety. This connection between a single mineral and both physical and mental health highlights just how integrated our nutritional needs are with our overall well-being.

Finding the Right Balance

When discussing micronutrients, balance is key. While deficiencies can lead to various health issues, overconsumption can be equally harmful. The modern diet, particularly in parts of the world where supplements and fortified foods are common, can sometimes tip the balance towards excess. For example, consuming too much vitamin A, especially in supplement form, can lead to toxicity, causing symptoms like dizziness, nausea, and in extreme cases, liver damage.

This brings us to an important point: context matters. The best way to ensure you're getting the right balance of vitamins and minerals isn't necessarily through pills and powders, but through a varied, whole-foods-based diet. Nature has an elegant way of packaging nutrients in the right proportions, with whole fruits, vegetables, grains, and proteins providing not just vitamins and minerals, but the fiber, antioxidants, and other compounds that help the body absorb and utilize them effectively. For instance, eating an orange provides not just vitamin C, but also the fiber and phytonutrients that work synergistically to support health in ways that isolated vitamin C supplements cannot replicate. In some cases, supplementation is necessary— pregnant women often need more folic acid, the elderly may require additional B12 or vitamin D, and those with specific health conditions might benefit from targeted nutrients. But for most people, eating a diet rich in colorful fruits and vegetables, lean proteins, whole grains, and healthy fats will provide a robust array of the micronutrients needed for optimal health.

Micronutrients and Long-Term Health

Beyond their immediate functions, vitamins and minerals also play a crucial role in preventing chronic diseases. Antioxidant vitamins like C and E help protect the body from oxidative stress, which contributes to the aging process and the development of conditions like heart disease, diabetes, and cancer. Meanwhile, minerals like potassium and magnesium help regulate blood pressure, reducing the risk of heart disease.

While it might be tempting to think of nutrition in terms of macronutrients—proteins, carbs, and fats—the reality is that micronutrients are just as important, if not more so, for maintaining long-term health. They are the subtle architects of wellness, quietly ensuring that every system in the body has the tools it needs to function properly. In the end, the foundation of healthy eating isn't just about calories or macros; it's about nurturing your body with a wide array of essential nutrients, vitamins, and minerals included. And while they may be small in size, their impact on your health is nothing short of profound.

1.5 THE GUT-BRAIN CONNECTION: HOW DIGESTION AFFECTS MOOD AND WELL-BEING

Imagine, for a moment, that your body is a bustling city. Your gut, a sprawling metropolis, is constantly humming with activity—digesting food, absorbing nutrients, and managing waste. Now imagine that far away, in the nerve-filled, synapse-sparking capital of the body—your brain—a seemingly separate world of thoughts, emotions, and decisions is in play. But, in reality, these two distant "cities" are connected by an intricate superhighway known as the gut-brain axis. For years, we believed the brain dictated much of what happened in the body, like an all-knowing mayor issuing orders. However, recent research has flipped this narrative on its head, revealing that the gut and brain are in constant communication, often influencing each other in profound, unexpected ways. This connection is more than just a physical pathway; it's a dynamic, two-way dialogue. Signals from your brain can affect the functioning of your gut, but equally, the health of your gut can shape how you think, feel, and even respond to stress. The idea that "you are what you eat" has never rung truer, especially when we delve into how our digestive health impacts our mood and well-being.

The Microbiome: A Hidden World of Influence

At the heart of this gut-brain relationship is the microbiome—a community of trillions of bacteria, viruses, and fungi living within your digestive system. It's not an exaggeration to say that these microorganisms can play a pivotal role in your mental health. They are more than just passive inhabitants; they actively participate in the body's vital processes, including digestion, immune system regulation, and even the production of neurotransmitters—chemicals like serotonin and dopamine that are key players in your mood and emotional state.

Serotonin, in particular, stands out as a major player in the gut-brain conversation. While many think of serotonin as the "feel-good" chemical produced in the brain, what often surprises people is that around 90% of the body's serotonin is actually produced in the gut. This means that disturbances in gut health, such as inflammation or imbalances in the microbiome, can directly impact serotonin levels and, by extension, your mood. It's a concept so powerful that scientists have dubbed the gut your "second brain." What happens in your gut doesn't stay in your gut; it reverberates throughout your entire system.

Consider a time when you felt "butterflies" in your stomach before an important event or experienced digestive discomfort during a period of intense stress. This is the gut-brain connection in action. Your brain is sending signals to your digestive system, and in turn, the gut is responding. But the reverse is also true—an imbalance in your gut can send distress signals to your brain, potentially leading to anxiety, depression, or a feeling of unease that seems difficult to shake.

Stress and the Gut: A Feedback Loop

Stress is one of the most profound factors that can influence the gut-brain relationship. When you're under stress—whether it's from work, relationships, or even something as simple as juggling too many daily tasks—your body releases a cascade of stress hormones like cortisol. These hormones can alter digestion, slow down the absorption of nutrients, and even lead to uncomfortable symptoms like bloating or cramps. It's not just a temporary disruption, either. Chronic stress can lead to long-term changes in gut function, fostering an environment where harmful bacteria thrive, tipping the balance of the microbiome away from the diverse, healthy ecosystem it should be.

What's particularly fascinating, though, is that this relationship is not a one-way street. Just as stress can influence your gut, poor gut health can exacerbate stress levels. Inflammation in the gut, for example, can lead to the production of cytokines—proteins that trigger inflammation in other parts of the body, including the brain. These inflammatory signals can contribute to feelings of fatigue, sadness, or anxiety. What starts as a gut issue can quickly snowball into a full-body experience of emotional and physical distress.

Think of it as a feedback loop: stress impacts your gut, and gut issues can heighten your stress, creating a cycle that can be tough to break. This is why it's crucial not just to manage stress externally through relaxation techniques or therapy, but also internally—by supporting gut health through a balanced diet, adequate hydration, and nurturing your microbiome with prebiotics and probiotics.

How Food Affects Your Mood

While the gut-brain connection can seem complex and almost mystical, it boils down to some simple, tangible truths: what you put in your body affects how you feel. The foods you eat provide more than just fuel; they shape the environment of your gut, which in turn shapes your mental and emotional state.

Take, for example, a diet high in processed foods and refined sugars. These foods can create inflammation in the gut, throwing off the delicate balance of good and bad bacteria. Inflammation in the gut is increasingly being linked to mood disorders like depression and anxiety. This is because inflammation triggers the production of harmful molecules called cytokines, which can cross the blood-brain barrier and influence brain function, leading to cognitive fog, low energy, and feelings of sadness or irritability. It's a sobering thought, but one worth considering when we think about the standard Western diet and its potential role in the rising rates of mental health issues.

On the flip side, a diet rich in whole foods—fruits, vegetables, lean proteins, healthy fats—can foster a healthy, diverse microbiome. Fiber-rich foods, in particular, are a favorite of gut bacteria. These bacteria ferment fiber in the large intestine, producing short-chain fatty acids that have been shown to have anti-inflammatory effects not just in the gut, but throughout the body, including the brain. Essentially, a healthy gut can help quell inflammation, supporting clearer thinking and a more balanced emotional state.

Fermented foods like yogurt, kefir, sauerkraut, and kimchi also deserve a special mention. These foods are rich in probiotics—live beneficial bacteria that can help replenish and support your microbiome. Adding these foods to your diet can be a simple yet powerful way to improve gut health, which in turn can lead to a better mood, improved focus, and greater emotional resilience.

Beyond Food: Nurturing the Gut-Brain Connection

While diet plays a starring role in the gut-brain connection, it's not the only factor that matters. Sleep, exercise, and stress management all contribute to a healthy gut and a healthy mind. Inadequate sleep, for instance, can disrupt your gut's bacterial balance, leading to the same kinds of issues that poor diet can cause. This is why chronic sleep deprivation often leads to irritability, mood swings, and even depression.

Exercise, meanwhile, has been shown to have a positive effect on gut health. Moderate, regular physical activity can increase microbial diversity, reduce inflammation, and even improve the body's ability to metabolize food effectively. It's another example of how interconnected our body's systems are—what's good for one part of the body is often good for another.

As for stress, learning to manage it effectively can be a game-changer for your gut health. Mindfulness practices, deep breathing, and other relaxation techniques can help calm the nervous system and reduce the release of stress hormones that disrupt gut function. It's a feedback loop worth investing in: as your stress levels drop, your gut becomes healthier, which in turn supports a calmer, more balanced mind.

A Holistic Approach to Well-being

In a world where we're constantly bombarded with quick fixes and miracle diets, it's easy to overlook the importance of the fundamentals.

But the gut-brain connection reminds us that true well-being is holistic—it's not just about what you eat, but how you feel, how you move, and how you manage the stresses of life. The conversation between your gut and your brain is constant, and while we may not always be conscious of it, its effects are profound. By paying attention to this connection, we can make choices that nurture both our physical health and our emotional well-being. Supporting your gut through mindful eating, stress management, and self-care doesn't just improve digestion—it can transform your entire sense of balance, calm, and happiness.

CHAPTER 2: BREAKING FREE FROM DIET MYTHS
2.1 COMMON WEIGHT LOSS MYTHS DEBUNKED

As we embark on this journey of enlightened eating and lifestyle modification, it's crucial to clear the mist around some of the most pervasive myths in the world of weight loss. These myths often deter good intentions, leading to frustration and setbacks in your health goals. Let's explore these misconceptions, understand why they're misleading, and reaffirm your path to sustainable weight management. Each myth unraveled here is based on current scientific understanding and practical experience in dietary science.

Firstly, one of the most common traps many fall into is the belief that **"extreme calorie restriction leads to faster weight loss."** This approach may yield immediate results, but it's unsustainable and potentially harmful in the long term. When you drastically cut down your calorie intake, your body goes into survival mode, slowing metabolism to conserve energy. Over time, this not only makes it more difficult to lose weight but can also lead to muscle loss, nutritional deficiencies, and a weakened immune system. Instead, focus on a balanced diet where calorie intake supports daily energy needs without excess.

Another widespread myth is that **"all fats are bad."** The truth is, your body needs fat — the right kind of fat. Healthy fats found in avocados, nuts, seeds, and certain oils like olive and canola, play a vital role in heart health, absorption of vitamins, and overall cellular function. What's crucial is differentiating these beneficial fats from the saturated and trans fats found in processed foods, which can raise bad cholesterol levels and increase the risk of heart disease.

Moving on, many believe that **"carbohydrates make you gain weight."** Carbs, much like fats, are not inherently bad despite their bad reputation. They are a primary energy source, especially crucial for brain function and physical activity. Problems arise with the type and quantity of carbohydrates consumed. Refined carbs such as white bread, pastries, and other highly processed foods can indeed contribute to weight gain and metabolic issues when eaten in excess. However, whole grains, fruits, and vegetables are carbohydrate sources that provide essential nutrients and fiber, promoting fullness and improved metabolic health.

It's also often touted that **"supplements can replace meals."** While supplements can help cover nutrient deficiencies, they should not be considered a substitute for the variety of nutrients available from whole foods. Whole foods provide an array of nutrients along with dietary fiber, which supplements lack. Relying heavily on supplements can lead to imbalances and miss essential components of a healthy diet that supports long-term weight management and health.

Furthermore, **"eating late at night causes weight gain"** is another myth that needs addressing. It's not necessarily the timing of eating, but what and how much we eat that matters. Consuming a large, heavy meal right before bed can affect sleep quality and digestion, but a small, nutrient-dense snack can actually be part of a well-balanced diet. Listening to your body's hunger cues and choosing healthy snacks is key, rather than the time on the clock.

An equally misleading belief is that **"weight loss is a linear process."** Weight loss often involves fluctuations—an initial drop followed by periods of plateau or even slight gains, which reflect normal body processes. Factors such as fluid retention, muscle gain, and hormonal changes can all influence scale weight. Thus, it's important to gauge progress through a combination of metrics that include, but are not limited to, weight—such as energy levels, fit of your clothes, and overall sense of well-being.

Lastly, the notion that **"diet foods are the best choices for weight loss"** can be deceptive. Labels like "low-fat" or "sugar-free" can be enticing but these products often contain high levels of artificial sweeteners, refined flours, and other additives to enhance taste and texture, which can derail your health goals. Instead, gravitate towards whole, minimally processed foods that naturally contain the nutrients you need with none of the misleading claims.

By debunking these myths, we pave the way toward a more informed approach to weight loss—one that champions balance, variety, and moderation in your diet. Remember, a nourishing diet that fits your lifestyle is the cornerstone of maintaining a healthy body weight and improving overall health. Keep these clarifications in mind as you make daily choices, ensuring that your efforts in shedding pounds are based on truths that align with your body's needs and the latest in nutritional science.

2.2 Why Fad Diets Fail: What You Really Need to Know

In your journey toward achieving a healthier lifestyle and weight loss, the allure of fad diets can be tempting. They promise rapid results with minimal effort, which on the surface seems ideal when you're looking to make a significant change swiftly. However, understanding why these diets often fail to deliver long-term success is crucial for anyone seeking sustainable health improvements.

Fad diets usually come with the appeal of immediate and dramatic results. They often propose a radical change in eating patterns—usually by excluding certain types of foods or nutrients perceived as 'bad', such as carbohydrates in ketogenic diets or fats in low-fat diets. The problem with this approach lies not in reducing calorie intake, which can indeed lead to weight loss, but in the unsustainable nature of extreme restrictions.

Consider the case of Emma, a dedicated professional with two kids. Like many, she found herself seeking quick weight loss solutions after a holiday season filled with indulgence. She opted for a juice cleanse—an increasingly popular fad diet characterized by consuming only fruit and vegetable juices for days or weeks at a time. Initially, the pounds seemed to melt away, but Emma quickly found herself struggling with low energy, difficulty concentrating, and immense cravings for solid foods. Not only did this diet disrupt her social and family life, being unable to share meals, but once she resumed her normal diet, the weight she had lost returned swiftly, bringing along a few extra pounds for the rebound.

This example underscores a vital flaw in many fad diets: the pendulum swing. When you restrict your body of essential nutrients or overall calorie intake to an extreme, it's not unusual for the body to respond by lowering its metabolic rate as a protective measure against starvation. What's more, the psychological impact of drastic dietary restrictions can lead to a significant increase in cravings for the very foods you're avoiding, often resulting in binge-eating behaviors once the diet phase is over.

Moreover, fad diets are typically low in complexity regarding nutritional balance. They fail to provide an array of nutrients from different food sources, which are integral to our overall health. This can lead to serious deficiencies that might not manifest until much later. Without the right balance of carbohydrates, proteins, fats, vitamins, and minerals, our bodies cannot function optimally. Physical symptoms such as hair loss, weakened nails, and skin issues, alongside fatigue and decreased immune function, can all arise from prolonged adherence to such diets.

Another significant issue with fad diets is their one-size-fits-all approach. Nutritional needs can be profoundly personal, varying according to age, gender, activity level, and existing health conditions. A diet that works wonders for one person might be detrimental to another. For instance, while a low-carb diet might benefit someone with specific metabolic issues, it might cause problems for another who performs high-intensity workouts regularly.

Sustainability is another critical factor. Fad diets do not teach long-term eating habits. They focus on short-term changes and quick fixes rather than cultivating a healthy relationship with food. True dietary success lies in making incremental changes that can be sustained over time, not just over weeks or months. Adopting eating patterns that are balanced culturally, socially, and nutritionally can promote health without causing feelings of deprivation or isolation.

The psychological aspect of eating is as important as the physiological effects of food on our bodies. Fad diets often ignore the social and emotional components of eating. Meals are not merely about ingesting nutrients but are rituals for family bonding, socializing, and satisfaction. Diets that do not consider these aspects are likely to fail because eating behavior is complex and influenced by many factors beyond simple hunger.

In conclusion, while the quick fixes promoted by fad diets may seem appealing, they often set you up for failure and disappointment. For weight loss and health improvements to be sustainable, they must be approached through a balanced diet that accommodates personal preferences, lifestyle, and nutritional needs. This approach ensures not only the achievement of desired weight goals but also the maintenance of overall health and well-being in the long run. By understanding and accepting these dynamics, you are more likely to reject the transient allure of fad diets and embrace a more balanced, enjoyable, and healthful eating strategy that stands the test of time.

2.3 BUILDING A DIET MINDSET FOR SUSTAINABLE SUCCESS

As we delve further into the world of true wellness and body positivity, the next step beyond debunking harmful myths is crafting a mindset that embraces diet as a part of a holistic lifestyle rather than a periodic or extreme change. It's about developing a perspective that fosters life-long habits of healthy eating, understanding that quick fixes don't equate to lasting wellness. This involves cultivating attitudes and beliefs that support sustainable changes, understanding the deep-seated nature of our food choices, and adapting our behaviors for long-term success.

Creating a diet mindset isn't primarily about strict adherence to nutritional rules, but about forming a genuine, mindful connection with what we eat. It involves shifting from a diet-centric view where certain foods are vilified, and eating schedules are rigidly controlled, to a more nourishing approach that listens to your body's needs, respects its signals, and nourishes it without guilt or punishment.

Consider Martha, a graphic designer with a bustling freelance career who juggled her profession and her role as a mom. Martha had tried numerous diets: some demanded cutting out carbs, others insisted on liquid-only meals for days. Each diet ended the same way—she would initially lose weight but would eventually revert to old eating habits, leading each time to frustration and self-blame. Her breakthrough came when she shifted her mindset from dieting to nourishing her body. She started focusing on why she was eating, rather than merely what or how much she was eating. This shift gave her the freedom to choose foods not only for their nutritional value but for their role in her overall health and well-being.

Embracing Nutritional Flexibility

One key aspect of building a sustainable diet mindset is embracing flexibility. Rigid dietary rules can lead to a restrictive mindset, which can create a negative relationship with food, often characterized by guilt and deprivation. Instead, understanding that it's okay to occasionally indulge in favorite foods can lead to greater satisfaction and can actually reduce cravings and overeating.

Cultivating Mindful Eating Habits

Another component is mindful eating, which involves paying full attention to the experience of eating and drinking, both inside and outside the body. It helps you tune into physical hunger and satiety cues, slowing down the eating process, and allowing yourself to savor and enjoy your meals without distraction. This way, Martha learned to recognize when she was truly hungry and when she was eating out of boredom, stress, or emotional discomfort.

Prioritizing Moods and Food

The psychological aspect of eating cannot be overlooked in the quest to build a lasting diet mindset. Often, emotional states heavily influence our food choices; stress, sadness, or even extreme happiness can lead us to overeat or indulge in less nutritious foods. By recognizing these patterns, you can start to develop healthier coping mechanisms for managing emotions, such as engaging in physical activity, meditating, or other hobbies that beneficially distract from immediate food impulses.

Setting Realistic Goals

Setting achievable and realistic goals is fundamental. Instead of aiming for quick, drastic changes (like losing 20 pounds in a month), setting goals such as improving overall physical health, gaining more energy, or reducing junk food intake by half within a month can be more effective. These goals are not only realistic but also help cultivate patience and resilience in your dietary journey, aligning with the fact that sustainable health is a long-term commitment.

Celebrating Non-Scale Victories

A significant shift in the diet mindset is moving away from the scale. While weight can be a measure of health, it isn't the only one. Non-scale victories, such as better sleep, improved skin condition, higher energy levels, enhanced mood, and better physical stamina, can also be powerful motivators and indicators of your commitment to a healthier lifestyle.

Continuous Learning and Adaptation

Finally, maintaining a flexible approach to new information is crucial. Nutritional science evolves constantly, and being open to adapting your eating habits in light of new research is part of a sustainable diet mindset. This doesn't mean chasing every new diet trend, but rather, assessing new information as it comes, incorporating changes that suit your body's needs, and always putting your well-being at the forefront of dietary choices. In conclusion, building a diet mindset that promotes sustainable success is about more than following a set of strict nutritional guidelines.

It is about creating a flexible, mindful, and informed approach to eating that recognizes the comprehensive role food plays in our lives, far beyond mere sustenance. Like Martha, shifting from a temporary, restrictive dieting paradigm to an enriched, enduring approach to eating can transform how you view nutrition and lead to lasting health and well-being.

CHAPTER 3: NUTRITION ESSENTIALS FOR BUSY LIVES

3.1 SIMPLE MEAL PREP TECHNIQUES FOR TIME-SAVING SUCCESS

In the whirlwind of daily life, with its urgent meetings and endless to-do lists, finding time to prepare healthy, nourishing meals can often feel like a race against the clock. Imagine, then, the possibility of transforming your kitchen rituals in a way that not only saves time but also enhances your wellness journey. This vision is not only attainable; it's necessary for anyone looking to maintain a healthy diet amidst a busy schedule. Take Julia, for example, a full-time marketing executive and mother of two, who found meal prepping to be a game-changer for her hectic lifestyle. Sunday afternoons, previously a scramble to manage chores and prepare for the work week, have now become her meal prep golden hours. She uses this time to chop vegetables, cook proteins, and portion out balanced meals into containers that are ready to grab and go. This routine not only streamlines her week but also ensures that she and her family have access to healthy meals every day.

The Cornerstones of Efficient Meal Prep

The essence of effective meal prep lies in its strategic approach. The first step is to appreciate the variations of meal prepping. Some prefer to prepare entire meals that are ready to be reheated, while others might just prep parts of meals, like chopping veggies or cooking a large batch of quinoa. Understanding your personal preference can dramatically tailor your approach to suit your lifestyle.

Another key component is selecting the right recipes. Opt for dishes that are both satisfying and simple to prepare. Dishes that freeze well or can be made in large batches, like soups, stews, or casseroles, are perfect. They not only save time but also preserve the quality and taste of the ingredients.

Balancing Variety and Consistency

The challenge, however, lies in maintaining both variety and nutrition. Eating the same meal several days in a row can become monotonous, and it's often where meal prep loses its charm. To counter this, Julia integrates a mix of interchangeable components—grilled chicken, roasted veggies, a variety of grains like brown rice or barley—that can be mixed and matched to create different meals throughout the week. This strategy not only keeps the menu interesting but also covers a wide array of nutrients. Indeed, variety is the spice of life, and in the context of meal prepping, it's also the secret to nutritional balance. Each meal component can be seen as a building block, contributing its unique flavor and health benefits to an overarching goal of well-being.

Tools of the Trade

Investing in quality kitchen tools can also revolutionize the meal prep process. High-powered blenders, durable chopping tools, and spacious mixing bowls make the prep work quicker and more efficient. Similarly, having a set of reliable containers of various sizes for storing prepped ingredients or whole meals is crucial. These containers not only organize your fridge but also make it visually appealing, encouraging you to stay on track with your health goals.

Time Management: The Real Hero

Effective time management plays a pivotal role in meal prepping. Allocating a specific block of time each week for meal prep is essential. This not only creates a routine but also ensures that meal prepping doesn't become an overwhelming chore. Additionally, leveraging cooking methods that allow for multitasking—like baking or slow cooking—can free you up to focus on other tasks while still making progress in the kitchen.

Embracing Flexibility

However, it's important to remember that flexibility is key. Life is unpredictable, and rigid plans can sometimes add more stress than they alleviate. Julia recalls a week where an impromptu client dinner threatened to derail her meal plan. Instead of seeing it as a setback, she used it as an opportunity to enjoy a break from the routine, confident in her ability to return to her prepped meals the next day.

This flexibility extends to adjusting meal prep methods over time. What works one month might need tweaking the next. Listening to your body's needs and responding to your schedule can help refine the process, making it a sustainable part of your lifestyle, rather than a burdensome task.

The Psychological Boost

An often-overlooked benefit of meal prepping is its psychological impact. Knowing that your meals are planned and ready can significantly reduce daily decision fatigue and stress. For many, like Julia, this preparation becomes more than just a time-saver; it's a mental health booster, providing peace of mind that dietary choices are taken care of. Moreover, the act of taking time to prepare your meals can also reinforce a commitment to health and can be a form of self-care. It is a moment in the week dedicated to ensuring you are nourished and energized—an investment in your health and well-being.

Conclusion

In the end, simple meal prep techniques are not just about saving time—they're about transforming your approach to eating and lifestyle management. They empower you to make healthier choices, reduce daily stress, and enjoy a variety of nutritious meals despite the demands of a busy life. Meal prepping is an adaptable tool, evolving with your needs and daily life pressures but always providing a foundation for healthy eating. By adopting some of these practices, anyone, regardless of how packed their schedule looks, can turn the tide in their favor, making mealtime an ally in their quest for health and vitality.

3.2 SMART GROCERY SHOPPING: WHAT TO BUY AND WHAT TO AVOID

Picture yourself navigating the grocery store, your cart empty and your mind full of the countless options lining the shelves. This place can either be a gateway to health or a tricky labyrinth where diet traps lurk around every corner. Smart grocery shopping isn't just about choosing fresh produce over packaged goods; it's about knowing which staples will sustain your healthy eating plan and which temptations to resist. Let's stroll through the aisles with Emma, a pediatric nurse with a bustling career and three active kids. Her weekly challenge? Filling her cart with nutritious foods that meet the tastes and health needs of a busy family, while sidestepping those sneaky, unhealthy choices.

Mastering the Perimeter

Emma's strategy starts with mastering the layout of her local store. Like many savvy shoppers, she sticks primarily to the store's perimeter. Here she finds the essentials: fruits, vegetables, fresh meats, and dairy products. These periphery sections of the grocery store typically house the freshest and least processed foods. By filling most of her cart here, Emma ensures her family's diet is based around whole foods, rich in nutrients necessary for maintaining energy and health.

Navigating the Inner Isles

However, even the most health-conscious shopper can't avoid the inner aisles altogether. This is where grains, cooking oils, and other staples reside. Emma's approach is targeted; she knows what she needs. Her list usually includes whole grains like quinoa and brown rice, almond butter, and canned legumes, all versatile ingredients that support her meal planning. She smartly bypasses the aisles with sugary cereals and snacks, reducing the temptation to splurge on less healthy options.

Labels: The Truth-Tellers

When venturing beyond the perimeter to the middle aisles, Emma pays close attention to food labels. Food labels can be revealing but also misleading. Emma has learned how to decode them. She checks serving sizes, sugar contents, and the list of ingredients, avoiding products with ingredients she can't pronounce. This simple rule of thumb helps her choose products that are as close to their natural state as possible.

Organic or Not?

Another question Emma faces is whether to go organic. She follows a basic rule: for high-consumption foods and those known to have higher pesticide residues, like apples, strawberries, and spinach, she opts for organic. For others, such as avocados and bananas, she feels comfortable buying the conventional versions. This approach balances cost and dietary preferences without compromising on her family's exposure to pesticides.

Seasonal and Local

Emma also focuses on seasonal and local produce when available. These options are not only fresher and tastier but also more economical and environmentally friendly. They frequently come from nearby farms, supporting local agriculture and reducing the carbon footprint associated with long-distance transportation. This practice feeds her family better while also nurturing the community and the planet.

Avoiding the Allure of Convenience

In an age where every grocery store is brimming with convenience meals—from frozen dinners to pre-cut fruit—Emma steers clear. She knows these options aren't just more expensive; they often contain preservatives and excessive sodium. Instead, she invests time at home prepping these meals and snacks. Doing so, she controls the ingredients, ensuring that her family's meals are healthy and tailored to their tastes.

Bulk Buying Wisdom

For non-perishable items and staples, Emma turns to bulk buying, which offers both economic and environmental benefits. She purchases larger quantities of items like brown rice, nuts, and dried beans, reducing both packaging waste and trips to the grocery store. However, she's careful to store these bulk items properly to maintain their freshness and nutritional quality.

The Checkout Strategy

Finally, as Emma approaches the checkout, where snacks and sugary treats are strategically placed to tempt shoppers, she keeps her resolve. Her cart, filled with thoughtfully chosen, nutritious items, reflects her commitment to her family's health. This checkout line becomes not just the end of her shopping trip but a testament to her successful navigation of the grocery landmines.

Conclusion

Smart grocery shopping, as Emma demonstrates, is a skill refined over time. It starts with a plan, informed by an understanding of where healthful options reside and a commitment to resisting less beneficial ones. It's about making choices that align with long-term goals for health and well-being, not just immediate gratification or convenience. Emma's shopping habits ensure that her kitchen is a foundation of health, supplying the fuel her active family needs to thrive.

In the journey toward a more health-conscious lifestyle, the path might begin at the grocery store, but it flourishes in the decisions we make there. Each smart choice is a step toward lasting wellness, empowering us to build healthier lives, one item at a time.

3.3 Eating Out and Staying on Track: Tips for Restaurants and Social Events

Imagine the scene: you're seated at a cozy table in your favorite restaurant, the atmosphere is buzzing, and you're about to catch up with old friends. Dining out and attending social events are among life's greatest pleasures, providing a chance to unwind, indulge, and socialize. However, for those focused on maintaining a healthy diet, these occasions can pose significant challenges. How does one navigate a menu smartly or socialize at events without derailing dietary goals? Let's walk through some practical strategies. Take Michael, a software developer and father, who once struggled to balance social engagements with his fitness goals. He loved dining out but often found himself either overindulging or feeling like he was missing out. That was until he developed a simple yet effective system to enjoy social outings without compromise.

Choosing the Right Locations

Michael's first trick lies in the choice of venue. Whenever possible, he suggests restaurants that he knows offer a range of healthy options or are willing to accommodate special dietary requests. For instance, places that highlight farm-to-table concepts or those with a clear emphasis on fresh produce can significantly ease the difficulty of sticking to health-conscious choices.

Pre-Plan the Order

Before heading out, Michael looks up the restaurant's menu online. This practice allows him to peruse the options at leisure, without the pressure of a waiter hovering for his order or friends chiming in with their less-health-conscious preferences. He decides what to eat in advance, making it less likely he'll make a spur-of-the-moment decision influenced by hunger or temptation.

Starting Right

Once at the restaurant, how he starts his meal also matters. Michael often orders a water or unsweetened iced tea to keep himself hydrated and to prevent confusing thirst with hunger. He also opts for a healthy appetizer, like a salad or broth-based soup, to curb his appetite and reduce the likelihood of overeating when his main course arrives.

Customizing Meals

Don't hesitate to ask for modifications, Michael advises. Simple requests such as dressing on the side, grilled instead of fried, or substituting a side salad for fries, are generally accommodated without fuss. These small tweaks ensure that his meal remains within the boundaries of his dietary plan.

Mindful Eating

During the meal, Michael practices mindful eating—savoring each bite, putting down his cutlery between bites, and engaging in conversation. This mindfulness allows him to listen to his body's satiety cues, preventing overeating while also enhancing his dining experience by truly relishing the flavors and the company.

Handling Social Events

When it comes to larger social events such as weddings or parties, where buffet-style meals are common, Michael employs a different set of tactics. He makes it a point to survey all the options before filling his plate. This full-view approach helps him to strategically select foods that align with his goals while still allowing him the pleasure of partaking in the event's offerings.

He fills half his plate with vegetables, a quarter with lean proteins, and the remainder with whole grains or another nutrient-rich option. By constructing his plate in this manner, he ensures a balanced meal that satisfies without excess.

Indulging Intelligently

Michael believes in the 90/10 rule—eating healthily 90% of the time and allowing himself the occasional indulgence. When dining out or celebrating a special occasion, he doesn't shy away from a slice of cake or a glass of wine, but he does so in moderation, savoring these moments rather than succumbing to guilt.

After the Meal

If the meal was particularly heavy, Michael doesn't beat himself up—instead, he plans a little extra physical activity for the next day or commits to eating lighter meals. This balanced approach ensures that a night out doesn't turn into a diet derailment.

Conclusion

In Michael's journey, the essence of successfully dining out and attending social gatherings without compromising his health goals lies in planning, mindfulness, and moderation. By applying these principles, any social setting can be navigated with confidence, allowing enjoyment without guilt or consequence. Eating out and socializing are integral parts of life, offering joys that shouldn't be overshadowed by dietary restrictions. With thoughtful strategies, these moments can be both pleasurable and in line with one's health aspirations, proving that balance isn't just possible—it's entirely attainable.

CHAPTER 4: MANAGING CRAVINGS AND EMOTIONAL EATING

4.1 UNDERSTANDING EMOTIONAL TRIGGERS AND OVERCOMING STRESS EATING

In our journey to healthier living, one of the most subtle yet compelling hurdles we encounter is the maze of our own emotions. Emotional triggers and stress eating are not simply about lacking control or willpower; they're deeply intertwined with our psychological makeup and daily experiences. Understanding this intricate relationship is the first step toward mastering it, empowering us to make better nutritional choices and foster a truly balanced life. Imagine coming home after a tough day at work. The boss was demanding, deadlines were looming, and your email wouldn't stop buzzing. You're greeted not just by the comfort of your sofa but, more tempting, the kitchen. For many of us, the kitchen is a refuge but also a place of challenge. Without realizing it, the stress of your day nudges you toward the fridge or the cookie jar. This isn't weakness—it's a natural response to emotional triggers.

The Psychology Behind Stress Eating

Stress eating, or emotional eating, is a coping mechanism. It's our body's attempt to mitigate stress with the quick 'fix' of comfort foods, which are often high in sugar, fat, and calories. Biologically, this makes sense; these foods temporarily boost serotonin levels, the brain's feel-good neurotransmitter, giving us a fleeting sense of relief. The crux of the struggle with stress eating lies in its fleeting nature. The relief is temporary, and the underlying emotions remain unaddressed. This can create a cycle where emotions drive poor eating habits, only to be followed by guilt and further emotional distress. It is this cycle we aim to break.

Recognizing Your Emotional Triggers

Identifying personal emotional triggers is a crucial step. Emotional triggers are specific moments, interactions, or feelings that prompt an emotional response leading to stress eating. For instance, some might find that a heated conversation can send them straight toward snack-driven solace. For others, boredom or feelings of loneliness might be the catalyst. Keeping a food and mood diary can be an effective tool to identify these triggers. By documenting not just what and how much you eat, but also your emotions before and after eating, patterns will emerge. This self-awareness is a powerful first weapon in your arsenal against stress eating.

Strategies to Overcome Stress Eating

Once you recognize the patterns, you can begin to implement strategies to combat them. Here are several approaches that blend practicality with psychological insight:

- **Mindful Eating**: This involves being fully present during meals, savoring each bite, and acknowledging your feelings and sensations. Mindful eating encourages you to notice flavors, textures, and smells, and most importantly, to listen to your hunger cues. It's about enjoying your food but also recognizing when you are full, helping to prevent overeating driven by emotions rather than hunger.

- **Stress Management Techniques**: Since stress is a primary trigger for emotional eating, managing stress proactively can help curb the impulse. Techniques like meditation, deep breathing exercises, yoga, or even regular physical activity can significantly reduce stress levels. Engaging in hobbies that you enjoy or finding humor in daily situations can also serve as excellent stress relievers.

- **Healthy Alternatives**: When the urge to eat emotionally strikes, it can be helpful to have healthy alternatives at hand. Instead of reaching for ice cream or chips, consider foods that are satisfying but also good for you. For instance, a mix of nuts, a piece of dark chocolate, or a bowl of fresh berries can fulfill your craving without the negative consequences of more indulgent foods.

- **Emotional Support**: Sometimes, the best antidote to emotional eating is talking through your feelings with someone you trust. Whether it's a friend, family member, or therapist, sharing can lighten your emotional load and reduce the urge to handle it through eating. Additionally, joining support groups where members share similar experiences can provide comfort and practical advice.

Implementing Long-Term Changes

Implementing these strategies requires patience and commitment. Changes will not happen overnight, but with consistency, they will become part of your routine. As you practice these new habits, you'll find yourself not only eating better but feeling better. Remember, overcoming stress eating isn't just about cutting calories or losing weight—it's about understanding and managing your emotions.

By addressing emotional triggers directly, you enhance your overall wellbeing, paving the path to a healthier, more balanced life. In this ongoing journey of health and self-discovery, each step you take towards understanding your emotional landscape is a step towards not just a healthier diet, but a richer, more fulfilled life. It's about feeding not just your body, but also your soul—nurturing yourself with each choice, and finding that balance and harmony between taste, nourishment, and emotional freedom.

4.2 HEALTHY SNACK ALTERNATIVES FOR CURBING CRAVINGS

Navigating through the day-to-day demands of modern life, we often find ourselves between meetings, errands, and activities, facing the mighty cravings that abruptly enter our minds like unwelcome guests. These cravings don't just test our resolve; they can derail our carefully thought-through eating plans. How do we handle these without slipping? The solution lies in having an array of healthy snack alternatives ready to combat these cravings effectively and deliciously.

Imagine you're working late; the glow of your computer screen is the only light in the room. Suddenly, you realize you're hungry—not just regular hungry, but the kind that leads you to contemplate devouring anything in sight. This moment is critical, and your choice of snack can set the tone for your entire evening and perhaps your nutritional habits moving forward.

Why Cravings Strike: A Biological Glimpse

Understanding why we crave certain foods is a fascinating blend of biology and psychology. Often, when we're stressed, our bodies expend more energy, resulting in increased hunger and specific cravings. Sugary and fatty foods release serotonin, temporarily making us feel better. However, these spikes are transient and can leave us feeling worse thereafter.

On a biological level, cravings can also stem from a lack of nutrients in our regular diets. When the body yearns for a quick energy boost or a way to uplift our mood, it naturally craves items that are instantly gratifying. The problem arises when the instant fix leads to long-term setbacks in our diet plans.

Choosing the Right Snack: A Blend of Taste and Health

The art of choosing the right snack involves balancing satisfaction with health.

Let us explore how this balance can be achieved without compromising taste or convenience:

- **Fruit-Based Treats**: Fruits are nature's candies, rich in fibers, vitamins, and natural sugars, providing a sweet fix without the guilt. A well-portioned mix of berries, an apple, or a banana can offer the immediate satisfaction of sweetness coupled with fiber, which slows down the absorption of sugar, avoiding the pitfalls of energy spikes and crashes.
- **Nuts and Seeds**: A handful of nuts or seeds can be an excellent way to stave off hunger. Almonds, walnuts, and chia seeds, for example, not only provide a crunchy texture that can offset cravings for less healthy snack options but also contribute essential fatty acids and protein, which help in satiety.
- **Healthy Fats and Proteins**: Avocados or hummus paired with vegetables like carrots or cucumber slices provide a satisfying creamy texture and flavor. The blend of healthy fats and proteins helps in keeping you fuller for longer, reducing the likelihood of overindulging later.
- **Yogurt and Smoothies**: Greek yogurt or plant-based alternatives topped with a sprinkle of nuts and a drizzle of honey can quench the desire for something creamy and sweet. Smoothies blending greens with a touch of fruit offer rejuvenation without excessive calories.

Strategic Snacking: Timing and Portions

Equally important as choosing a healthy snack is knowing when to snack and how much. Understanding your body's signals and differentiating between genuine hunger and mere boredom or stress is crucial. Implementing structured snacking – planned snacks at specific times – can prevent both overeating at meals and indulging in unhealthy options. Portion control is paramount. Preparing single-serving snack portions ahead of time or purchasing pre-packaged healthy snacks can help manage quantities consumed. This proactive approach removes the temptation to overeat directly from larger packets or containers.

Integrating Snacks into Your Lifestyle

Let's redefine snacking. It's not just an act of eating between meals but an integral part of a holistic diet, contributing to our overall energy and nutrient intake.

Here's how you can integrate healthy snacking seamlessly into your lifestyle:

- **Keep It Varied**: Rotate your snack options to prevent boredom and ensure a range of nutrients. This not only keeps the palate interested but also benefits different aspects of health by diversifying the nutrients your body receives.

- **Accessibility is Key**: Make healthy snacks as accessible as possible. Keep them at your workstation, in your car, or in your bag. The easier they are to reach, the less likely you are to opt for less healthy alternatives.

- **Blend With Your Daily Routine**: Associate snacks with certain parts of your day. A fruit or a protein bar could be your afternoon routine, perhaps taking a break from your desk while enjoying a yogurt could become a part of your morning ritual.

Emotional and Physical Balance

By choosing healthier snacks, we're not just feeding our bodies but also nurturing our minds. Avoid the emotional pitfalls of guilt associated with unhealthy snacking. Healthy options provide not just physical nourishment but emotional satisfaction, knowing you made a choice that supports your overall well-being. Being prepared with healthy snacks is empowering—it puts you in control of your cravings, rather than letting them control you. As we progress through our pursuit of health, remember, each snack is not just a small meal; it's a building block towards a healthier lifestyle. Crafting this mindful approach to snacking enriches not only your diet but enhances your relationship with food as a source of nourishment and joy.

4.3 MINDFUL EATING: HOW TO STAY PRESENT DURING MEALS

As we embark on the journey toward a holistic sense of health and well-being, one key practice emerges as both profoundly simple and surprisingly powerful: mindful eating. It's about bringing our full attention to the experiences and sensations of eating, transforming mealtime from mere nourishment into a moment of deep self-connection and awareness. In this way, each meal becomes an opportunity to reinforce our commitment to good health, to pause in the midst of our busy lives, and truly engage with the food that sustains us. Visualize a typical dinner at home: You might be eating while scrolling through your phone, watching TV, or planning the day ahead. It's easy to finish a meal without really tasting it, without appreciating the textures and flavors, or even acknowledging how much you have consumed. Now, imagine transforming this experience into one where each bite is acknowledged, savored, and appreciated. This is the essence of mindful eating.

The Philosophy and Practice of Mindful Eating

Mindful eating is rooted in mindfulness, a practice that comes from ancient meditative traditions and has been adapted in the modern world as a tool to reduce stress and enhance quality of life. At its core, mindfulness involves maintaining a moment-by-moment awareness of our thoughts, feelings, bodily sensations, and surrounding environment. When applied to eating, mindfulness means paying full attention to the experience of eating and drinking, both inside and outside the body. It involves noticing the colors, smells, textures, and flavors of food, as well as the mind's response to these sensations. Eating becomes an intentional act, rather than an automatic or mindless one.

The Benefits of Mindful Eating

The benefits of adopting this approach are manifold. Firstly, it helps in regulating appetite, as paying attention to every bite tends to slow down the pace of eating, which in turn gives the body the time it needs to recognize satiety and reduce the likelihood of overeating. Furthermore, when we eat mindfully, we are more likely to make healthier food choices, as we are fully conscious of what and how much we are eating. On a deeper level, this practice can transform our relationship with food. It turns eating into a practice of self-care, where food is viewed not just as sustenance, but as a source of pleasure and nourishment. It encourages a profound appreciation of food's journey before it reaches the plate, enhancing gratitude for the Earth's resources, the farmers who nurture the crops, and the cooks who prepare the meals.

Integrating Mindful Eating into Daily Life

Incorporating mindful eating into your daily routine doesn't have to be daunting. It can start with small, manageable steps:

1. **Begin with Silence**: Start each meal with a moment of silence or a deep breath. This simple act can help center your thoughts and focus your mind on the meal ahead.

2. **Eliminate Distractions**: Turn off the TV, put away electronic devices, and clear away books or papers. By removing distractions, you allow yourself to fully engage with the experience of eating.

3. **Engage All Your Senses**: Before you begin to eat, take a moment to appreciate the appearance and aroma of your food. As you eat, pay attention to the texture of the food, the flavor in every bite, and the sounds of your surroundings.

4. **Appreciate Each Bite**: Chew slowly, and try to savor each mouthful. This not only aids digestion but also allows you to derive maximum satisfaction from your meal.

5. **Check-In with Your Body**: Periodically during your meal, pause to ask yourself how full you are. This helps prevent eating past the point of feeling comfortably satiated.

6. **Acknowledge Your Effect on the Environment**: Consider the environmental impact of your food choices. Mindful eating also involves awareness of how your consumption affects the world around you, fostering a more sustainable approach to living.

Challenges and Overcoming Them

Initially, adopting a mindful eating practice might feel awkward or forced. The key is consistency and patience. Like any form of exercise, the 'muscles' of mindfulness need to be trained and developed over time. Start small, perhaps with one mindful meal a week, and gradually increase as it becomes more natural.

You might face setbacks—moments of forgetfulness, meals eaten in haste, days when mindfulness seems like too much effort. These are all natural parts of the learning curve. What's important is returning to the practice, meal after meal, day after day.

The Ripple Effects of Mindful Eating

Mindful eating has the potential to extend beyond the dining table into other areas of life, fostering a general presence that can enhance relationships, work, and play. It encourages a state of active, open attention on the present, which enriches every aspect of daily life.

By cultivating mindfulness during our meals, we nurture a sense of respect for our bodies and gratitude for the nourishment we receive. This gratitude can spill over, enhancing feelings of well-being and contentment. Mindful eating teaches us that every meal, every bite, is an opportunity to connect deeply with our bodies, our food, and our world. It's a practice not just of eating, but of living.

CHAPTER 5: SUPERCHARGING YOUR DIET WITH NUTRIENT-DENSE FOODS

5.1 INCORPORATING SUPERFOODS FOR OPTIMAL HEALTH

Imagine walking through a vibrant market, each stall bursting with colors that seem to shout the promise of better health. There's a kaleidoscope of fruits, vegetables, and other thrilling superfoods, each with a story to tell and a benefit to offer. Today, we will uncover those stories hidden within superfoods and explore how integrating them into your diet can lead to optimal health and vitality. Superfoods, though not scientifically defined, are considered the elite players on your nutritional team. These foods are nutrient powerhouses, providing vitamins, minerals, antioxidants, and other health-enhancing properties. In this journey toward a rejuvenated lifestyle, let's look at how these extraordinary foods fit into the puzzle of a healthy diet.

First, let's demystify what makes a food "super." It's all about nutrient density. Spinach, for example, offers more than just iron; it's a splendid source of vitamins A, C, K, and several B vitamins, not to mention its wealth of minerals and fiber—all with minimal calories. Contrast this with foods high in calories but low in nutrients, and you'll see why spinach earns its superfood status. Another champion in the realm of superfoods is berries. Blueberries, strawberries, and raspberries aren't just delightful and refreshing—they are a powerhouse of antioxidants, which help combat oxidative stress that contributes to aging and chronic diseases. The narrative of these small fruits includes their mighty fight against large adversaries—chronic conditions.

Equally compelling is the story of nuts and seeds. Walnuts, chia seeds, and flaxseeds offer not just crunch and texture but also significant amounts of omega-3 fatty acids, crucial for heart health and anti-inflammatory effects. Integrating these into your diet can be as simple as sprinkling them over a salad or blending them into your morning smoothie, making nutrition both effortless and enjoyable. Now, consider quinoa, a seed that masquerades as a grain. This versatile superfood contains all nine essential amino acids, making it a complete protein—a rare plant-based nutrient composition that's a boon for vegetarians and meat-eaters alike. Its mild, nutty flavor makes it an excellent base for a variety of dishes, embodying the principle of versatility meeting nutrition. Let's not forget about the superheroes of the vegetable world: kale and broccoli. These vegetables stand out due to their high content in vitamins C, K, and A, and for good reason. They offer powerful glucosinolates, chemicals that have been studied for their cancer-preventing potential. Integrating these vegetables into your diet creates an environment where health can thrive amid the challenges posed by modern diets.

Not only do superfoods play crucial roles in health and wellness directly by offering their bounty of nutrients, but they also influence your overall dietary patterns. Their rich flavors and satisfying textures make healthier eating a pleasurable experience. They naturally crowd out less nutritious foods, subtly shifting your diet towards something that is not only sustainable but also enjoyable.

Imagine a typical day infused with these superfoods. Your breakfast could start with a smoothie made from kale, berries, and a touch of almond butter. For lunch, a quinoa salad topped with sliced almonds and chunks of roasted sweet potato. Dinner could be a hearty stir-fry featuring broccoli, bell peppers, and lean protein like chicken or tofu. Snacks? Dates filled with nut butter or small handfuls of trail mix with dark chocolate and dried berries.

Incorporating superfoods isn't just about adding specific items to your shopping list. It's about considering the synergy of your overall diet. How do these foods interact? Are you balancing superfoods with a good variety of all food groups? Remember, the aim here is not just to sprinkle a few extra seeds on your dish now and then. The goal is weaving a tapestry of varied, colorful, and nutrient-dense foods that come together to form a holistic diet.

This approach also helps address common barriers and challenges in maintaining an optimal diet. For instance, the simplicity of using versatile superfoods such as spinach or blueberries lessens the time required for meal preparation, aligns with your busy schedule, and naturally displaces the less healthy choices that might tempt you during a hurried lunch break or late-night snack time.

As you embark on this journey of integrating superfoods into your lifestyle, remember that each small choice contributes to a larger narrative of health. It's not about perfection but progression. It's about making better choices more often. The incorporation of superfoods into your diet builds not just meals but a foundation for a healthier, more vibrant life.

Embrace these nutritional champions as part of your everyday eating habits, and watch as their benefits transform your health narrative from one of short-term dieting to lifelong wellness. This is the true art of eating well—making choices that naturally lead to better health without making you feel like you're on a restrictive diet. After all, it is a lifestyle nourished by the rich stories and profound benefits hidden within our foods—and isn't that a delightful way to live?

5.2 BALANCING YOUR PLATE: HOW TO GET ALL YOUR ESSENTIAL NUTRIENTS

Picture your plate as a canvas, its contents an array of colors and textures, each contributing not just to your meal's visual appeal, but also to your body's complex nutritional needs. Achieving a balanced diet is akin to painting this canvas every day, using a palette of nutrients that supports optimal health and vitality. Here, we explore how to ensure every meal leads not only to culinary enjoyment but to holistic nourishment. Understanding the balance of nutrients begins with envisioning the perfect plate at mealtimes. Imagine dividing this plate into sections, each portioned to fit the macronutrients—the proteins, carbohydrates, and fats—and a generous splash of micronutrients from various fruits and vegetables.

Proteins, vital for cell repair and growth, should ideally make up a quarter of your plate. Your protein sources can weave in a narrative of variety, ranging from lean meats and poultry to rich legumes and tempeh. Each type of protein not only nourishes your body but brings its own set of secondary benefits, like the fiber in beans and the healthy fats in fish such as salmon.

Next, consider the **carbohydrates**. Often unfairly vilified in diet culture, these are your body's primary energy suppliers. About a quarter of your plate should include whole grains like brown rice, quinoa, or whole-wheat pasta. These grains bring more than just energy; they come loaded with fiber, helping digestion and prolonging the feeling of fullness, an essential aspect of weight management.

Half of your plate should be reserved for fruits and vegetables—the paint strokes that bring vibrant colors and vital nutrients to your meal. Including a wide variety of colors can be a practical guide to getting a broad range of antioxidants and vitamins.

Dark, leafy greens, bright bell peppers, deep blueberries, and sunny oranges each carry unique compounds that support different aspects of health, from reducing inflammation to enhancing immune function.

Fats are also crucial, despite their reputation. They should be thought of as a condiment rather than a main component. A drizzle of olive oil on a salad or a sprinkle of chopped nuts on a dish is an adequate representation. These fats are necessary for optimal brain health and the absorption of fat-soluble vitamins like A, D, E, and K, proving that fats, when chosen wisely and used sparingly, are not foes but friends. It's also essential to tailor this balance to your life's rhythms and demands. For someone with an active lifestyle, including more carbohydrates might be necessary to sustain energy levels. For others, higher protein intake might be essential to support muscle repair and growth. Listening to your body and adjusting your nutrient intake accordingly is the artistry behind personal nutrition.

Harmonizing this nutrient balance also means understanding that no single meal has to be perfectly compartmentalized. Nutritional balance is achieved over time. A lunch lighter in vegetables might lead you to prepare a veggie-rich dinner. The flexibility in managing your meals is like mixing colors on a palette—sometimes blending, sometimes contrasting, but always creating a coherent whole by day's end.

The beauty of this approach lies not only in its simplicity but in its flexibility. As seasons change, so does the availability of various foods, and with that, your plate's landscape. Summer might bring an abundance of fresh berries and fruits, making it easier to fill half of your plate with raw, refreshing produce. Winter might shift your focus to root vegetables and hearty soups, which also ensures that you get a broad spectrum of nutrients year-round. Moreover, understanding how to balance your meals opens the door to a deeper connection with your food. Knowing the origins of your meal's components, such as the farmland where your vegetables grew or the ocean waters your fish came from, can add a layer of appreciation and consciousness to your dining experience. Visualizing your diet as a dynamic equilibrium, where the give and take of nutrient types flow with the days and seasons, empowers you to create meals that are not only satisfying but also deeply nourishing. This approach liberates you from the confines of strict dieting paradigms and introduces you to the more sustainable practice of eating well by choice and with pleasure.

In closing, balance should not be a static metric but a fluid, easily adaptable approach that respects your body's needs, the demands of your life, and the seasonality of foods. This kind of mindful eating emphasizes that every meal is an opportunity to nourish not just the body but also the soul, fostering a relationship with food that is both healthful and joyous. As you continue this journey, remember that each plate is a reflection of your health intentions, painted with the brushstrokes of your dietary choices.

5.3 SUPPLEMENTS: WHICH ONES TO CONSIDER AND WHY

In our journey toward enhanced wellness and vitality, even the most carefully crafted diet might sometimes fall short of meeting every nutritional necessity. This is where the story of dietary supplements begins—a narrative that supports and complements your diet when certain nutrients are not sufficiently supplied through food alone.

Supplements should not be the protagonists in your health story, but rather supporting characters that fill gaps and ensure your body's nutritional screenplay is complete. Picking the right ones, however, requires understanding both their roles and the specific chapters of your life where they might be needed the most.

Imagine a scene where you have been trying to increase your iron intake through diet alone. You've added spinach, lentils, and red meat to your daily meals, yet you still feel the symptoms of iron deficiency like a lingering fatigue clouding your day. This could be a cue for a carefully chosen iron supplement, playing a supportive role in your body's energy production and overall vitality. But remember, before adding any supplement to your regimen, consider consulting with a healthcare provider to ensure it's a fitting addition to your personal health script.

Vitamin D is another commonly considered supplement, particularly for those in climates with limited sunshine or individuals who spend major portions of their day indoors. Known as the 'sunshine vitamin,' Vitamin D is vital for bone health, immune function, and even mood regulation. If the natural production of Vitamin D via sunlight is limited, a supplement might just shine a light, fostering stronger bones and a spirited immune system. Then, consider omega-3 fatty acids, found abundantly in fish like salmon and sardines, which many might not consume regularly. These fats are crucial for cognitive health, cardiovascular wellness, and reducing inflammation throughout the body. If fish frequently finds itself off your plate, supplementing omega-3s might just craft a more heartening tale of health for you.

For those exploring plant-based diets, B12 is a critical chapter not to be skimmed over. Since Vitamin B12 is primarily found in animal products, those who do not consume these might encounter a plot twist in their nutrition story—a deficiency. Here, a B12 supplement isn't just helpful; it's essential for maintaining energy levels, proper nerve function, and production of DNA and red blood cells.

Moreover, storytelling around dietary choices often includes chapters about specific life stages or conditions, such as pregnancy or osteoporosis. In these instances, folate supplements are crucial characters for pregnant individuals, playing a preventive role against spinal cord defects in developing babies. Calcium and Vitamin D become significant actors in preserving bone density as the narrative of age includes twists of potential osteoporosis. While discussing the ensemble of potential supplements, it's also important to acknowledge the role of probiotics. These supplements, thriving with beneficial bacteria, support a gut-friendly plot twist, enhancing digestive health and bolstering the immune system. If your diet lacks fermented foods like yogurt, sauerkraut, or kefir, probiotics might step in to support your gut's health subplot. Transitioning this ensemble into your daily script does require caution, though. More is not always better in the realm of supplementation. Each body character in your health story processes nutrients differently, and excessive doses of supplements can sometimes lead to adverse effects, turning a well-intentioned subplot into a cautionary tale. Consistent, open dialogue with healthcare professionals can ensure that supplements enhance rather than complicate your health narrative. Lastly, be mindful of quality. The supplement market is vast and variably regulated, which means product quality can vary dramatically. Opting for brands that voluntarily submit their products for independent testing can add a layer of trust and assurance, keeping your story both safe and beneficial. Consider supplements as an adjunct or a supporting cast to your well-rounded diet—not the lead actors. By doing so, you align both diet and supplementation to your body's unique requirements, crafting a holistic narrative that speaks to sustained health and vitality. This approach isn't just about swallowing pills but making informed, mindful decisions that bolster the chapters of your ongoing wellness journey.

CHAPTER 6: 10 WEEK MEAL PLAN FOR LASTING RESULTS

6.1 WEEK 1: JUMPSTART YOUR METABOLISM WITH CLEAN EATING

WEEK 1	breakfast	snack	lunch	snack	dinner
Monday	Power Protein Smoothie Bowl	Almond and Chia Energy Balls	Mediterranean Chickpea Salad	Avocado and Egg Toast	Grilled Salmon with Asparagus and Quinoa
Tuesday	Sunrise Tofu Scramble	Greek Yogurt with Mixed Nuts and Seeds	Grilled Chicken Hummus Wrap	Spiced Chickpea Crunchies	Herb-Roasted Chicken with Zucchini and Tomatoes
Wednesday	Chia and Berry Parfait	Roasted Chickpeas with Paprika	Spinach and Quinoa Power Salad	Tofu and Veggie Mini Frittatas	Lentil and Veggie Stew with Brown Rice
Thursday	Omega Boost Smoothie	Kale Chips with Nutritional Yeast	Creamy Vegan Broccoli Soup	Greek Yogurt and Berry Parfait	Baked Cod with Roasted Brussels Sprouts and Sweet Potatoes

Friday	Smoked Salmon and Avocado Omelet	Pomegranate Quinoa Salad	Zesty Quinoa and Black Bean Salad	Cucumber Mint Refresh	Chicken and Veggie Sheet Pan Dinner
Saturday	Spinach & Feta Egg Muffins	Almond Butter & Berry Rice Cakes	Grilled Vegetable and Hummus Wrap	Quick Cottage Cheese and Pineapple Bowl	One-Pan Turmeric Tofu & Chickpeas
Sunday	Peanut Butter Banana Overnight Oats	Tuna-Stuffed Avocado Boats	Spicy Turkey and Avocado Wrap	No-Bake Berry Cashew Cream Bars	Spicy Shrimp and Broccoli Stir-Fry

6.2 WEEK 2: HIGH-PROTEIN, LOW-CARB MEAL STRATEGIES

WEEK 2	breakfast	snack	lunch	snack	dinner
Monday	Smoked Salmon and Avocado Omelet	Smoked Salmon and Avocado Roll-Ups	Grilled Chicken Hummus Wrap	Roasted Chickpeas with Paprika	Grilled Salmon with Asparagus and Quinoa
Tuesday	Almond Flour Pancakes	Almond Butter and Berry Energy Balls	Tuna Avocado Salad Sandwich	Avocado and Egg Toast	Turkey and Veggie Stir-Fry

Wednesday	Kale and Mushroom Scramble	Greek Yogurt with Mixed Nuts and Seeds	Spicy Turkey and Avocado Wrap	Pomegranate Quinoa Salad	Herb-Roasted Chicken with Zucchini and Tomatoes
Thursday	Chia and Coconut Breakfast Pudding	Tofu and Veggie Mini Frittatas	Egg Salad Lettuce Wraps	Quick Cottage Cheese and Pineapple Bowl	Baked Cod with Roasted Brussels Sprouts and Sweet Potatoes
Friday	Simple Tofu Scramble	Spiced Chickpea Crunchies	Hummus Veggie Wrap with Quinoa	Tuna-Stuffed Avocado Boats	Lentil and Veggie Stew with Brown Rice
Saturday	Spinach & Feta Egg Muffins	Almond Butter & Berry Rice Cakes	Mediterranean Chickpea Salad	Almond Butter & Berry Rice Cakes	Chicken and Veggie Sheet Pan Dinner
Sunday	Peanut Butter Banana Overnight Oats	Greek Yogurt and Berry Parfait	Spinach and Quinoa Power Salad	No-Bake Berry Cashew Cream Bars	One-Pan Turmeric Tofu & Chickpeas

6.3 WEEK 3: DETOXING YOUR SYSTEM WITH WHOLE FOODS

WEEK 3	breakfast	snack	lunch	snack	dinner
Monday	Power Protein Smoothie Bowl	Greek Yogurt with Mixed Nuts and Seeds	Creamy Vegan Broccoli Soup	Almond and Chia Energy Balls	Lentil and Veggie Stew with Brown Rice
Tuesday	Chia and Berry Parfait	Pomegranate Quinoa Salad	Zesty Quinoa and Black Bean Salad	Avocado and Egg Toast	Herb-Roasted Chicken with Zucchini and Tomatoes
Wednesday	Omega Boost Smoothie	Kale Chips with Nutritional Yeast	Grilled Vegetable and Hummus Wrap	Greek Yogurt and Berry Parfait	Grilled Tofu with Sautéed Kale and Quinoa
Thursday	Sunrise Tofu Scramble	Almond Butter & Berry Rice Cakes	Mediterranean Chickpea Salad	Quick Cottage Cheese and Pineapple Bowl	Baked Cod with Roasted Brussels Sprouts and Sweet Potatoes
Friday	Peanut Butter Banana	Roasted Chickpeas with Paprika	Spinach and Quinoa Power Salad	No-Bake Berry Cashew Cream Bars	Spicy Shrimp and Broccoli Stir-Fry

	Overnight Oats				
Saturday	Smoked Salmon and Avocado Omelet	Tofu and Veggie Mini Frittatas	Grilled Chicken Hummus Wrap	Spiced Chickpea Crunchies	One-Pan Turmeric Tofu & Chickpeas
Sunday	Spinach & Feta Egg Muffins	Cucumber Mint Refresh	Egg Salad Lettuce Wraps	Tuna-Stuffed Avocado Boats	Grilled Salmon with Asparagus and Quinoa

6.4 WEEK 4: INCORPORATING HEALTHY FATS FOR SATIETY AND ENERGY

WEEK 4	breakfast	snack	lunch	snack	dinner
Monday	Almond Flour Pancakes	Almond Butter and Berry Energy Balls	Grilled Chicken Hummus Wrap	Tofu and Veggie Mini Frittatas	Herb-Roasted Chicken with Zucchini and Tomatoes
Tuesday	Chia and Coconut Breakfast Pudding	Smoked Salmon and Avocado Roll-Ups	Tuna Avocado Salad Sandwich	Avocado and Egg Toast	Baked Cod with Roasted Brussels Sprouts and Sweet Potatoes

Wednesday	Peanut Butter Banana Overnight Oats	Roasted Chickpeas with Paprika	Egg Salad Lettuce Wraps	Greek Yogurt and Berry Parfait	One-Pan Turmeric Tofu & Chickpeas
Thursday	Spinach & Feta Egg Muffins	Greek Yogurt with Mixed Nuts and Seeds	Hummus Veggie Wrap with Quinoa	No-Bake Berry Cashew Cream Bars	Grilled Tofu with Sautéed Kale and Quinoa
Friday	Smoked Salmon and Avocado Omelet	Almond Butter & Berry Rice Cakes	Spinach and Quinoa Power Salad	Tuna-Stuffed Avocado Boats	Lentil and Veggie Stew with Brown Rice
Saturday	Kale and Mushroom Scramble	Spiced Chickpea Crunchies	Mediterranean Chickpea Salad	Quick Cottage Cheese and Pineapple Bowl	Spicy Shrimp and Broccoli Stir-Fry
Sunday	Chia and Berry Parfait	Pomegranate Quinoa Salad	Grilled Vegetable and Hummus Wrap	Kale Chips with Nutritional Yeast	Chicken and Veggie Sheet Pan Dinner

6.5 WEEK 5: SMART PORTION CONTROL AND BALANCED MEALS

WEEK 5	breakfast	snack	lunch	snack	dinner
Monday	Power Protein Smoothie Bowl	Almond and Chia Energy Balls	Creamy Vegan Broccoli Soup	Avocado and Egg Toast	Herb-Roasted Chicken with Zucchini and Tomatoes
Tuesday	Sunrise Tofu Scramble	Kale Chips with Nutritional Yeast	Zesty Quinoa and Black Bean Salad	Tofu and Veggie Mini Frittatas	Lentil and Veggie Stew with Brown Rice
Wednesday	Chia and Berry Parfait	Greek Yogurt with Mixed Nuts and Seeds	Grilled Chicken Hummus Wrap	Greek Yogurt and Berry Parfait	Baked Cod with Roasted Brussels Sprouts and Sweet Potatoes
Thursday	Almond Flour Pancakes	Pomegranate Quinoa Salad	Egg Salad Lettuce Wraps	Quick Cottage Cheese and Pineapple Bowl	Spicy Shrimp and Broccoli Stir-Fry
Friday	Omega Boost Smoothie	Roasted Chickpeas with Paprika	Spinach and Quinoa Power Salad	No-Bake Berry Cashew Cream Bars	Grilled Tofu with Sautéed Kale and Quinoa

Saturday	Simple Tofu Scramble	Spiced Chickpea Crunchies	Tuna Avocado Salad Sandwich	Almond Butter & Berry Rice Cakes	Chicken and Veggie Sheet Pan Dinner
Sunday	Peanut Butter Banana Overnight Oats	Tuna-Stuffed Avocado Boats	Grilled Vegetable and Hummus Wrap	Pomegranate Citrus Infusion	Grilled Salmon with Asparagus and Quinoa

6.6 WEEK 6: INTERMITTENT FASTING TO BOOST WEIGHT LOSS

WEEK 6	breakfast	snack	lunch	snack	dinner
Monday	Chia and Coconut Breakfast Pudding	Greek Yogurt with Mixed Nuts and Seeds	Grilled Chicken Hummus Wrap	Avocado and Egg Toast	Herb-Roasted Chicken with Zucchini and Tomatoes
Tuesday	Almond Flour Pancakes	Almond Butter & Berry Rice Cakes	Tuna Avocado Salad Sandwich	Pomegranate Quinoa Salad	Grilled Tofu with Sautéed Kale and Quinoa
Wednesday	Peanut Butter Banana Overnight Oats	Kale Chips with Nutritional Yeast	Mediterranean Chickpea Salad	No-Bake Berry Cashew Cream Bars	Lentil and Veggie Stew with Brown Rice

Thursday	Power Protein Smoothie Bowl	Tofu and Veggie Mini Frittatas	Spinach and Quinoa Power Salad	Greek Yogurt and Berry Parfait	One-Pan Turmeric Tofu & Chickpeas
Friday	Smoked Salmon and Avocado Omelet	Roasted Chickpeas with Paprika	Grilled Vegetable and Hummus Wrap	Spiced Chickpea Crunchies	Chicken and Veggie Sheet Pan Dinner
Saturday	Spinach & Feta Egg Muffins	Almond Butter and Berry Energy Balls	Zesty Quinoa and Black Bean Salad	Quick Cottage Cheese and Pineapple Bowl	Spicy Shrimp and Broccoli Stir-Fry
Sunday	Kale and Mushroom Scramble	Cucumber Mint Refresh	Creamy Vegan Broccoli Soup	Tuna-Stuffed Avocado Boats	Grilled Salmon with Asparagus and Quinoa

6.7 WEEK 7: MAINTAINING CONSISTENCY WITH FLEXIBLE EATING

WEEK 7	breakfast	snack	lunch	snack	dinner
Monday	Sunrise Tofu Scramble	Almond Butter & Berry Rice Cakes	Egg Salad Lettuce Wraps	Avocado and Egg Toast	Herb-Roasted Chicken with Zucchini and Tomatoes
Tuesday	Chia and Berry Parfait	Greek Yogurt with	Grilled Chicken	Greek Yogurt and	Baked Cod with Roasted

		Mixed Nuts and Seeds	Hummus Wrap	Berry Parfait	Brussels Sprouts and Sweet Potatoes
Wednesday	Spinach & Feta Egg Muffins	Almond Butter and Berry Energy Balls	Spinach and Quinoa Power Salad	Quick Cottage Cheese and Pineapple Bowl	Grilled Tofu with Sautéed Kale and Quinoa
Thursday	Smoked Salmon and Avocado Omelet	Kale Chips with Nutritional Yeast	Tuna Avocado Salad Sandwich	No-Bake Berry Cashew Cream Bars	Chicken and Veggie Sheet Pan Dinner
Friday	Almond Flour Pancakes	Roasted Chickpeas with Paprika	Mediterranean Chickpea Salad	Tofu and Veggie Mini Frittatas	Lentil and Veggie Stew with Brown Rice
Saturday	Peanut Butter Banana Overnight Oats	Spiced Chickpea Crunchies	Creamy Vegan Broccoli Soup	Tuna-Stuffed Avocado Boats	Spicy Shrimp and Broccoli Stir-Fry
Sunday	Chia and Coconut Breakfast Pudding	Pomegranate Quinoa Salad	Zesty Quinoa and Black Bean Salad	Cucumber Mint Refresh	Grilled Salmon with Asparagus and Quinoa

6.8 WEEK 8: COMBATING PLATEAUS AND REASSESSING GOALS

WEEK 8	breakfast	snack	lunch	snack	dinner
Monday	Power Protein Smoothie Bowl	Almond Butter and Berry Energy Balls	Grilled Chicken Hummus Wrap	Avocado and Egg Toast	Herb-Roasted Chicken with Zucchini and Tomatoes
Tuesday	Chia and Coconut Breakfast Pudding	Greek Yogurt with Mixed Nuts and Seeds	Zesty Quinoa and Black Bean Salad	Tuna-Stuffed Avocado Boats	Baked Cod with Roasted Brussels Sprouts and Sweet Potatoes
Wednesday	Peanut Butter Banana Overnight Oats	Kale Chips with Nutritional Yeast	Mediterranean Chickpea Salad	Quick Cottage Cheese and Pineapple Bowl	Lentil and Veggie Stew with Brown Rice
Thursday	Smoked Salmon and Avocado Omelet	Roasted Chickpeas with Paprika	Egg Salad Lettuce Wraps	Greek Yogurt and Berry Parfait	Grilled Tofu with Sautéed Kale and Quinoa
Friday	Almond Flour Pancakes	Pomegranate Quinoa Salad	Grilled Vegetable and Hummus Wrap	Tofu and Veggie Mini Frittatas	Spicy Shrimp and Broccoli Stir-Fry

Saturday	Spinach & Feta Egg Muffins	Spiced Chickpea Crunchies	Spinach and Quinoa Power Salad	Almond Butter & Berry Rice Cakes	One-Pan Turmeric Tofu & Chickpeas
Sunday	Kale and Mushroom Scramble	Cucumber Mint Refresh	Creamy Vegan Broccoli Soup	No-Bake Berry Cashew Cream Bars	Grilled Salmon with Asparagus and Quinoa

6.9 WEEK 9: BUILDING LONG-TERM HABITS FOR SUSTAINABLE SUCCESS

WEEK 9	breakfast	snack	lunch	snack	dinner
Monday	Chia and Berry Parfait	Almond and Chia Energy Balls	Grilled Chicken Hummus Wrap	Avocado and Egg Toast	Herb-Roasted Chicken with Zucchini and Tomatoes
Tuesday	Smoked Salmon and Avocado Omelet	Greek Yogurt with Mixed Nuts and Seeds	Mediterranean Chickpea Salad	Greek Yogurt and Berry Parfait	Baked Cod with Roasted Brussels Sprouts and Sweet Potatoes
Wednesday	Almond Flour Pancakes	Almond Butter & Berry Rice Cakes	Egg Salad Lettuce Wraps	Quick Cottage Cheese and	Lentil and Veggie Stew with Brown Rice

				Pineapple Bowl	
Thursday	Peanut Butter Banana Overnight Oats	Kale Chips with Nutritional Yeast	Spinach and Quinoa Power Salad	No-Bake Berry Cashew Cream Bars	Spicy Shrimp and Broccoli Stir-Fry
Friday	Spinach & Feta Egg Muffins	Roasted Chickpeas with Paprika	Grilled Vegetable and Hummus Wrap	Tuna-Stuffed Avocado Boats	Grilled Tofu with Sautéed Kale and Quinoa
Saturday	Kale and Mushroom Scramble	Tofu and Veggie Mini Frittatas	Tuna Avocado Salad Sandwich	Spiced Chickpea Crunchies	Chicken and Veggie Sheet Pan Dinner
Sunday	Chia and Coconut Breakfast Pudding	Pomegranate Quinoa Salad	Creamy Vegan Broccoli Soup	Cucumber Mint Refresh	Grilled Salmon with Asparagus and Quinoa

6.10 Week 10: Reflecting on Progress and Next Steps

WEEK 10	breakfast	snack	lunch	snack	dinner
Monday	Power Protein Smoothie Bowl	Almond Butter and Berry Energy Balls	Grilled Chicken Hummus Wrap	Avocado and Egg Toast	Herb-Roasted Chicken with Zucchini and Tomatoes
Tuesday	Sunrise Tofu Scramble	Greek Yogurt with Mixed Nuts and Seeds	Tuna Avocado Salad Sandwich	Greek Yogurt and Berry Parfait	Lentil and Veggie Stew with Brown Rice
Wednesday	Chia and Coconut Breakfast Pudding	Kale Chips with Nutritional Yeast	Spinach and Quinoa Power Salad	Quick Cottage Cheese and Pineapple Bowl	Grilled Tofu with Sautéed Kale and Quinoa
Thursday	Peanut Butter Banana Overnight Oats	Roasted Chickpeas with Paprika	Grilled Vegetable and Hummus Wrap	No-Bake Berry Cashew Cream Bars	Baked Cod with Roasted Brussels Sprouts and Sweet Potatoes
Friday	Almond Flour Pancakes	Pomegranate Quinoa Salad	Zesty Quinoa and Black Bean Salad	Tuna-Stuffed Avocado Boats	Spicy Shrimp and

					Broccoli Stir-Fry
Saturday	Spinach & Feta Egg Muffins	Spiced Chickpea Crunchies	Creamy Vegan Broccoli Soup	Almond Butter & Berry Rice Cakes	Chicken and Veggie Sheet Pan Dinner
Sunday	Smoked Salmon and Avocado Omelet	Cucumber Mint Refresh	Mediterranean Chickpea Salad	Tofu and Veggie Mini Frittatas	Grilled Salmon with Asparagus and Quinoa

CHAPTER 7: ENERGIZING BREAKFAST RECIPES FOR A HEALTHY START

7.1 High-Protein Breakfast Bowls and Smoothies

POWER PROTEIN SMOOTHIE BOWL

PREPARATION TIME: 10 min

COOKING TIME: 0 min

MODE OF COOKING: Blending

SERVINGS: 2

INGREDIENTS:

- 1 cup frozen blueberries
- 1 ripe banana
- 1/2 cup non-fat Greek yogurt
- 1/4 cup rolled oats
- 1 Tbsp chia seeds
- 1 Tbsp almond butter
- 1 cup spinach leaves
- 1/2 cup unsweetened almond milk

DIRECTIONS:

1. Combine blueberries, banana, Greek yogurt, oats, chia seeds, almond butter, spinach, and almond milk in a blender.
2. Blend on high until completely smooth and thick.
3. Pour into two bowls and smooth the top with a spoon.

TIPS:

- Top with a few additional chia seeds, sliced almonds, and fresh blueberry for extra crunch and flavor.
- If you prefer a thinner consistency, add a bit more almond milk before blending.

NUTRITIONAL VALUES: Calories: 295, Fat: 11g, Carbs: 36g, Protein: 14g, Sugar: 14g

SUNRISE TOFU SCRAMBLE

PREPARATION TIME: 5 min

COOKING TIME: 10 min

MODE OF COOKING: Sautéing

SERVINGS: 2

INGREDIENTS:

- 1/2 block firm tofu, crumbled
- 1 Tbsp olive oil
- 1/2 cup diced bell pepper
- 1/4 cup diced onions
- 1/2 tsp turmeric
- 1/2 tsp garlic powder

- Salt and black pepper to taste
- 2 Tbsp nutritional yeast
- 1/4 cup chopped fresh spinach

DIRECTIONS:

1. Heat olive oil in a skillet over medium heat.
2. Add bell peppers and onions, sautéing until soft.
3. Add crumbled tofu, turmeric, garlic powder, salt, and pepper. Stir to combine.
4. Cook for 5 minutes or until tofu is heated through and slightly crispy.
5. Stir in nutritional yeast and spinach, cooking until spinach is wilted.

TIPS:

- Serve over whole-grain toast or wrapped in a whole-grain tortilla for a heartier meal.
- Customize with additional veggies like mushrooms or tomatoes for more flavor and nutrients.

NUTRITIONAL VALUES: Calories: 180, Fat: 11g, Carbs: 8g, Protein: 12g, Sugar: 2g

PROTEIN-PACKED QUINOA & EGG BREAKFAST BOWL

PREPARATION TIME: 10 min

COOKING TIME: 20 min

MODE OF COOKING: Boiling/Sautéing

SERVINGS: 2

INGREDIENTS:

- 1/2 cup quinoa
- 1 cup water
- 2 Tbsp olive oil
- 4 eggs
- 1/2 avocado, sliced
- 1/2 cup cherry tomatoes, halved
- Salt and pepper to taste
- Optional garnish: chopped parsley

DIRECTIONS:

1. Rinse quinoa under cold water.
2. Bring water to a boil in a small pot, add quinoa, reduce heat to low, cover, and simmer for 15 minutes or until water is absorbed.
3. In a separate pan, heat 1 Tbsp olive oil over medium heat and fry eggs to your liking.
4. Divide quinoa into bowls. Top each bowl with two fried eggs, avocado slices, and cherry tomatoes.
5. Drizzle with remaining olive oil and season with salt and pepper.

Garnish with parsley if desired.

TIPS:

- Ensure quinoa is thoroughly rinsed to remove any bitterness.
- Cook eggs to your preference; over-easy or scrambled works well for this dish.

NUTRITIONAL VALUES: Calories: 410, Fat: 25g, Carbs: 30g, Protein: 20g, Sugar: 2g

---

CHIA AND BERRY PARFAIT

PREPARATION TIME: 15 min (plus soaking overnight)

COOKING TIME: 0 min

MODE OF

COOKING: Layering/Refrigerating

SERVINGS: 2

INGREDIENTS:

- 1/4 cup chia seeds
- 1 cup unsweetened almond milk
- 1 Tbsp honey or maple syrup
- 1/2 tsp vanilla extract
- 1 cup mixed berries (strawberries, blueberries, raspberries)
- 1/2 cup non-fat Greek yogurt

DIRECTIONS:

1. In a bowl, mix chia seeds with almond milk, honey, and vanilla extract. Stir well.
2. Cover and refrigerate overnight to allow chia seeds to expand.
3. The next morning, stir the chia pudding to ensure a uniform texture.
4. Layer chia pudding, yogurt, and mixed berries in two parfait glasses.

TIPS:

- For added texture, top with a sprinkling of granola.
- Can be prepared in advance for a quick and nutritious breakfast option.

NUTRITIONAL VALUES: Calories: 230, Fat: 9g, Carbs: 29g, Protein: 10g, Sugar: 18g

---

OMEGA BOOST SMOOTHIE

PREPARATION TIME: 5 min

COOKING TIME: 0 min

MODE OF COOKING: Blending

SERVINGS: 1

INGREDIENTS:

- 1/2 cup plain non-fat Greek yogurt
- 1 Tbsp flaxseeds
- 1/2 cup fresh spinach
- 1/2 banana
- 1/4 cup frozen raspberries
- 1/2 cup water or unsweetened almond milk
- 1 scoop protein powder (optional)

DIRECTIONS:

1. Place all ingredients into a blender.
2. Blend on high until smooth and creamy.

TIPS:

- Add ice for a thicker, frostier smoothie.

- If using protein powder, opt for an unflavored or vanilla variety to complement the fruit flavors.

NUTRITIONAL VALUES: Calories: 190, Fat: 4g, Carbs: 23g, Protein: 17g, Sugar: 12g

7.2 Low-Carb Breakfast Ideas for Sustained Energy

SMOKED SALMON AND AVOCADO OMELET

PREPARATION TIME: 10 min

COOKING TIME: 10 min

MODE OF COOKING: Sautéing

SERVINGS: 2

INGREDIENTS:

- 4 large eggs
- 1/2 avocado, sliced
- 4 oz. smoked salmon, sliced into strips
- 1 Tbsp extra virgin olive oil
- 1/4 tsp salt
- 1/4 tsp black pepper
- 1 Tbsp chopped fresh dill

DIRECTIONS:

1. Crack the eggs into a bowl, add salt and pepper, and beat until well mixed.
2. Heat the olive oil in a non-stick frying pan over medium heat.
3. Pour in the eggs and cook for 1-2 minutes until they begin to set on the bottom.
4. Arrange the smoked salmon and avocado slices evenly over one half of the omelet.
5. Sprinkle the chopped dill over the filling.
6. Carefully fold the other half of the omelet over the filling and cook for another 2-3 minutes.
7. Gently slide the omelet onto a plate and cut in half to serve.

TIPS:

• Ensure the pan is well-oiled to prevent sticking.

• Serve with a side of mixed greens for added fiber.

NUTRITIONAL VALUES: Calories: 290, Fat: 22g, Carbs: 3g, Protein: 20g, Sugar: 1g

ALMOND FLOUR PANCAKES

PREPARATION TIME: 10 min

COOKING TIME: 15 min

MODE OF COOKING: Frying

SERVINGS: 4

INGREDIENTS:

- 1 cup almond flour
- 2 large eggs
- 1/4 cup water
- 1 Tbsp coconut oil, melted
- 1 tsp baking powder
- 1/4 tsp salt
- Non-stick cooking spray or extra coconut oil for frying

DIRECTIONS:

1. In a large bowl, combine almond flour, baking powder, and salt.
2. In another bowl, whisk together eggs, water, and melted coconut oil.
3. Mix the wet ingredients into the dry ingredients until a batter is formed.
4. Heat a non-stick frying pan over medium heat and grease lightly with cooking spray or coconut oil.
5. Pour 1/4 cup of batter for each pancake and cook until bubbles form on the surface, about 2-3 minutes.
6. Flip and cook for an additional 1-2 minutes until golden brown.
7. Repeat until all batter is used.

TIPS:

- Add a small amount of vanilla extract or cinnamon for extra flavor.
- Almond flour can burn easily; keep the heat moderate.

NUTRITIONAL VALUES: Calories: 215, Fat: 18g, Carbs: 6g, Protein: 9g, Sugar: 1g

KALE AND MUSHROOM SCRAMBLE

PREPARATION TIME: 5 min

COOKING TIME: 10 min

MODE OF COOKING: Sautéing

SERVINGS: 2

INGREDIENTS:

- 4 large eggs
- 1 cup chopped kale
- 1/2 cup sliced mushrooms
- 1 Tbsp extra virgin olive oil
- Salt and pepper to taste
- 1/4 tsp garlic powder

DIRECTIONS:

1. Heat the olive oil in a non-stick skillet over medium heat.
2. Add the mushrooms and sauté for 3-4 minutes until softened.
3. Add the kale and cook until it wilts, about 2-3 minutes.
4. In a bowl, beat the eggs with salt, pepper, and garlic powder.
5. Pour the eggs over the vegetables

in the skillet and stir gently until the eggs are fully cooked.

6. Serve hot.

TIPS:

• Sprinkle some grated Parmesan cheese for added flavor.

• Serve with a slice of whole-grain toast if extra carbs are needed.

NUTRITIONAL VALUES: Calories: 190, Fat: 14g, Carbs: 4g, Protein: 12g, Sugar: 1g

CHIA AND COCONUT BREAKFAST PUDDING

PREPARATION TIME: 15 min (plus overnight chilling)

COOKING TIME: 0 min

MODE OF COOKING: No cook

SERVINGS: 2

INGREDIENTS:

• 1/4 cup chia seeds

• 1 cup unsweetened coconut milk

• 1 Tbsp coconut flakes

• 1/2 tsp vanilla extract

• 1 Tbsp almond butter

• Optional: Stevia or erythritol to taste

DIRECTIONS:

1. In a mixing bowl, combine the chia seeds, coconut milk, and vanilla extract.

2. If using, add sweetener to taste and mix thoroughly.

3. Divide the mixture between two

cups or mason jars.

4. Refrigerate overnight or at least 6 hours until the pudding has thickened.

5. Before serving, top with coconut flakes and a dollop of almond butter.

TIPS:

• Add a few berries on top for extra flavor and antioxidants.

• Stir a couple of times within the first hour of chilling to prevent clumping.

NUTRITIONAL VALUES: Calories: 200, Fat: 15g, Carbs: 10g, Protein: 4g, Sugar: 1g

SIMPLE TOFU SCRAMBLE

PREPARATION TIME: 5 min

COOKING TIME: 10 min

MODE OF COOKING: Sautéing

SERVINGS: 2

INGREDIENTS:

• 1 block (14 oz.) firm tofu, drained and crumbled

• 1 Tbsp extra virgin olive oil

• 1/2 tsp turmeric powder

• 1/2 cup chopped bell peppers

• 1/4 cup chopped onions

• Salt and pepper to taste

• 1 Tbsp nutritional yeast (optional)

DIRECTIONS:

1. Heat the olive oil in a non-stick

skillet over medium heat.

2. Add onions and bell peppers, sauté until tender, about 5 minutes.

3. Add the crumbled tofu and turmeric powder. Stir well to combine.

4. Cook for about 5-7 minutes, stirring often, until the tofu is heated through and slightly browned.

5. Season with salt, pepper, and nutritional yeast if using.

6. Serve hot.

TIPS:

• Add spinach or kale for extra greens.

• Great in a wrap or as a filling in an avocado half.

NUTRITIONAL VALUES: Calories: 250, Fat: 17g, Carbs: 6g, Protein: 20g, Sugar: 2g

7.3 Quick and Easy Make-Ahead Breakfast Options

Overnight Chia & Berry Oats

PREPARATION TIME: 10 min

COOKING TIME: 0 min (rest overnight)

MODE OF COOKING: Refrigeration

SERVINGS: 2

INGREDIENTS:

- 1 cup rolled oats
- 2 Tbsp chia seeds
- 1 cup unsweetened almond milk
- 1 cup mixed berries (fresh or frozen)
- 1 Tbsp almond butter
- 1 tsp vanilla extract
- Optional sweetener: 1 Tbsp honey or maple syrup

DIRECTIONS:

1. In a medium-sized mixing bowl, combine the rolled oats and chia seeds.

2. Add the almond milk, vanilla extract, and optional sweetener; mix well until combined.

3. Gently fold in the mixed berries and almond butter.

4. Divide the mixture between two mason jars or airtight containers.

5. Seal the containers and refrigerate overnight, allowing the oats and chia seeds to absorb the liquid and soften.

TIPS:

- If using frozen berries, there is no need to thaw them as they will defrost overnight.
- For added protein, stir in a scoop of vanilla or unflavored protein powder.

- Top with a few nuts or seeds for extra crunch and healthy fats right before serving.

NUTRITIONAL VALUES: Calories: 295, Fat: 9g, Carbs: 45g, Protein: 8g, Sugar: 12g

SPINACH & FETA EGG MUFFINS

PREPARATION TIME: 15 min

COOKING TIME: 20 min

MODE OF COOKING: Baking

SERVINGS: 6

INGREDIENTS:

- 6 large eggs
- 1/2 cup crumbled feta cheese
- 1 cup fresh spinach, chopped
- 1/4 cup red bell pepper, diced
- Salt and pepper to taste
- Non-stick cooking spray

DIRECTIONS:

1. Preheat your oven to 375°F (190°C).
2. Spray a muffin tin with non-stick cooking spray.
3. In a large bowl, beat the eggs. Add the chopped spinach, diced red bell pepper, and crumbled feta cheese. Season with salt and pepper, and mix well.
4. Pour the egg mixture evenly into the muffin tins, filling each about two-thirds full.
5. Bake in the preheated oven for 20 minutes, or until the tops are firm to the touch and eggs are cooked.
6. Allow to cool slightly before removing from the tin.

TIPS:

- These egg muffins can be stored in the refrigerator for up to 4 days.
- Reheat in the microwave for a quick and nutritious breakfast option.
- Add different vegetables like mushrooms or zucchini for variety.

NUTRITIONAL VALUES: Calories: 110, Fat: 7g, Carbs: 2g, Protein: 9g, Sugar: 1g

Peanut Butter Banana Overnight Oats

PREPARATION TIME: 10 min

COOKING TIME: 0 min (rest overnight)

MODE OF COOKING: Refrigeration

SERVINGS: 2

INGREDIENTS:

- 1 large ripe banana, mashed
- 1 cup rolled oats
- 1 Tbsp natural peanut butter
- 1 cup low-fat milk or almond milk
- 1 Tbsp chia seeds
- 1/2 tsp cinnamon

DIRECTIONS:

1. In a bowl, combine the mashed banana and peanut butter until smoothly mixed.
2. Add the rolled oats, chia seeds, cinnamon, and milk to the banana mixture and stir until well combined.
3. Divide the mixture into two mason jars or airtight containers.
4. Close the lids and refrigerate overnight, allowing the oats to soak up the flavors.

TIPS:

- Top with a few slices of fresh banana or a sprinkle of granola for added texture before serving.
- Ensure the peanut butter is well

stirred into the mixture to evenly distribute the flavor.

NUTRITIONAL VALUES: Calories: 320, Fat: 8g, Carbs: 50g, Protein: 10g, Sugar: 12g

Savory Quinoa Breakfast Bowl

PREPARATION TIME: 10 min

COOKING TIME: 15 min

MODE OF COOKING: Boiling

SERVINGS: 2

INGREDIENTS:

- 1 cup quinoa
- 2 cups water
- 1/2 cup cherry tomatoes, halved
- 1/2 avocado, diced
- 1/4 cup crumbled feta cheese
- 1 Tbsp olive oil
- Salt and pepper to taste
- 2 Tbsp fresh cilantro, chopped

DIRECTIONS:

1. Rinse the quinoa under cold water until the water runs clear.
2. In a medium pot, bring 2 cups of water to a boil. Add the quinoa, cover, and reduce heat to simmer for about 15 minutes or until all water is absorbed.
3. Remove from the heat and let it sit covered for 5 minutes; fluff with a fork.
4. Stir in the olive oil, salt, and

pepper.

5. Divide the cooked quinoa between two bowls. Top each with half the cherry tomatoes, diced avocado, crumbled feta, and chopped cilantro.

TIPS:

- Add a poached or soft-boiled egg on top for extra protein.
- Drizzle with a squeeze of fresh lime or lemon juice for added zest.

NUTRITIONAL VALUES: Calories: 290, Fat: 11g, Carbs: 39g, Protein: 9g, Sugar: 3g

APPLE-CINNAMON YOGURT PARFAIT

PREPARATION TIME: 10 min

COOKING TIME: 0 min

MODE OF COOKING: None

SERVINGS: 2

INGREDIENTS:

- 1 cup non-fat Greek yogurt
- 1 apple, cored and chopped
- 1/4 cup granola
- 1/2 tsp ground cinnamon
- 1 Tbsp honey (optional)

DIRECTIONS:

1. In two serving glasses or bowls, layer half the Greek yogurt at the bottom.
2. Add a layer of chopped apple and sprinkle with cinnamon.
3. Add a layer of granola and then repeat the layering with the remaining yogurt and apples.
4. Top with a final sprinkle of cinnamon and a drizzle of honey if desired.

TIPS:

- Choose a high-quality, low-sugar granola to keep this breakfast as healthy as possible.
- This parfait can be assembled the night before; just add the granola in the morning to maintain its crunch.

NUTRITIONAL VALUES: Calories: 190, Fat: 2g, Carbs: 34g, Protein: 10g, Sugar: 22g

CHAPTER 8: NOURISHING LUNCH RECIPES FOR WEIGHT LOSS

8.1 FRESH SALADS PACKED WITH NUTRIENTS AND FLAVOR

MEDITERRANEAN CHICKPEA SALAD

PREPARATION TIME: 20 min

COOKING TIME: 0 min

MODE OF COOKING: No heat preparation

SERVINGS: 4

INGREDIENTS:

- 2 cups canned chickpeas, drained and rinsed
- 1 cucumber, diced
- 1 bell pepper, diced
- 1 small red onion, finely chopped
- 1 cup cherry tomatoes, halved
- 1/4 cup kalamata olives, pitted and sliced
- 1/4 cup feta cheese, crumbled
- 1/4 cup extra virgin olive oil
- 2 Tbsp lemon juice
- 1 tsp dried oregano
- Salt and freshly ground black pepper, to taste

DIRECTIONS:

1. In a large bowl, combine chickpeas, cucumber, bell pepper, red onion, and cherry tomatoes.
2. Add kalamata olives and crumbled feta cheese to the bowl.
3. In a small bowl, whisk together olive oil, lemon juice, oregano, salt, and pepper.
4. Pour dressing over the salad and toss everything well to coat evenly.
5. Let the salad sit for about 10 minutes before serving to allow flavors to meld.

TIPS:

- Enhance this salad by adding freshly chopped parsley or mint for a burst of freshness.
- For best nutritional benefits, serve immediately or store in the refrigerator and consume within 24 hours.

NUTRITIONAL VALUES: Calories: 290, Fat: 17g, Carbs: 27g, Protein: 7g, Sugar: 5g

CRISPY TOFU AND VEGGIE TOSS

PREPARATION TIME: 15 min

COOKING TIME: 20 min

MODE OF COOKING: Sauteing and Baking

SERVINGS: 4

INGREDIENTS:

- 14 oz. extra firm tofu, pressed and cut into cubes
- 1 tbsp coconut oil
- 2 cups broccoli florets
- 1 red bell pepper, sliced
- 1 carrot, julienned
- 2 tbsp soy sauce
- 1 tbsp rice vinegar
- 1 tsp sesame oil
- 1 tsp ground ginger
- 1 garlic clove, minced
- Sesame seeds for garnish

DIRECTIONS:

1. Preheat oven to 400°F (204°C). Toss tofu cubes with coconut oil and spread on a baking sheet. Bake for 20-25 minutes until golden and crispy.
2. In a large pan, sauté broccoli, bell pepper, and carrot in sesame oil over medium heat for about 5-7 minutes.
3. In a small bowl, mix soy sauce, rice vinegar, ginger, and garlic.
4. Add baked tofu to the vegetables in the pan, pour the soy sauce mixture over, and toss to coat well.
5. Cook for an additional 2-3 minutes, letting the flavors meld.

TIPS:

- Pressing the tofu for at least 20 minutes before baking will result in firmer, crispier cubes.
- Serve over a bed of brown rice or quinoa for a heartier meal.

NUTRITIONAL VALUES: Calories: 195, Fat: 11g, Carbs: 14g, Protein: 12g, Sugar: 3g

SPINACH AND QUINOA POWER SALAD

PREPARATION TIME: 15 min

COOKING TIME: 15 min

MODE OF COOKING: Boiling

SERVINGS: 4

INGREDIENTS:

- 1 cup quinoa, rinsed
- 2 cups water
- 4 cups fresh spinach
- 1/2 cup cherry tomatoes, halved
- 1/2 avocado, sliced
- 1/4 cup sunflower seeds
- 1/4 cup red bell pepper, diced
- 2 Tbsp lemon juice
- 1 Tbsp extra virgin olive oil
- Salt and pepper to taste

DIRECTIONS:

1. In a medium saucepan, bring 2 cups of water to a boil. Add quinoa, reduce to a simmer, cover, and cook for 12-15 minutes or until water is

absorbed.

2. Fluff the quinoa with a fork and let cool for 5 minutes.

3. In a large bowl, combine the spinach, cherry tomatoes, avocado, sunflower seeds, and red bell pepper.

4. Add the cooled quinoa to the salad.

5. In a small bowl, whisk together lemon juice, olive oil, salt, and pepper.

6. Pour the dressing over the salad and toss gently.

TIPS:

- Add grilled chicken or tofu for extra protein.
- Store in an airtight container for a perfect lunch meal prep.

NUTRITIONAL VALUES: Calories: 320, Fat: 15g, Carbs: 35g, Protein: 10g, Sugar: 3g

8.2 Protein-Packed Wraps and Sandwiches for On-the-Go

GRILLED CHICKEN HUMMUS WRAP

PREPARATION TIME: 15 min
COOKING TIME: 10 min
MODE OF COOKING: Grilling
SERVINGS: 2
INGREDIENTS:

- 2 skinless chicken breasts
- 1 Tbsp extra virgin olive oil
- 1 tsp garlic powder
- Salt and pepper to taste
- 2 whole-grain tortillas
- 4 Tbsp hummus
- 1 cup mixed greens (spinach and arugula)
- 1/2 cucumber, thinly sliced
- 1 small carrot, julienned

PROCEDURE:

1. Preheat grill to medium-high heat (about 375°F or 190°C).

2. Rub the chicken breasts with olive oil, garlic powder, salt, and pepper.

3. Grill the chicken for about 5 min per side or until fully cooked and internal temperature reaches 165°F (74°C).

4. Let the chicken rest for a few minutes, then slice thinly.

5. Lay out the tortillas and spread each with 2 Tbsp of hummus.

6. Layer sliced chicken, mixed greens, cucumber slices, and carrot over the hummus.

7. Carefully roll the tortillas, folding in the sides to enclose the filling.

8. Cut each wrap in half and serve immediately.

TIPS:

- For extra flavor, add a few slices of avocado or a sprinkle of chili flakes.

- Keep wraps tightly covered with foil if taking on-the-go for fresher taste.

NUTRITIONAL VALUES: Calories: 380, Fat: 12g, Carbs: 34g, Protein: 36g, Sugar: 3g

---

TUNA AVOCADO SALAD SANDWICH

PREPARATION TIME: 10 min

COOKING TIME: 0 min

MODE OF COOKING: No Cook

SERVINGS: 2

INGREDIENTS:

- 1 can (5 oz.) tuna, drained
- 1 ripe avocado, mashed
- 1 Tbsp lemon juice
- 2 Tbsp chopped red onion
- Salt and pepper to taste
- 4 slices whole-grain bread
- 1/2 cup fresh arugula

PROCEDURE:

1. In a small bowl, combine the mashed avocado and lemon juice.

2. Add the drained tuna, chopped red onion, salt, and pepper to the avocado mixture and stir to combine well.

3. Toast the whole-grain bread slices lightly if desired.

4. Spread half of the tuna mixture onto a slice of bread, top with a handful of arugula, and cover with another slice.

5. Repeat with the remaining ingredients to make the second sandwich.

TIPS:

- Drizzle a little bit of flaxseed oil over the tuna mixture for added omega-3 fatty acids.

- The sandwich can be made ahead of time and stored in the refrigerator for a quick grab-and-go option.

NUTRITIONAL VALUES: Calories: 360, Fat: 15g, Carbs: 34g, Protein: 25g, Sugar: 5g

SPICY TURKEY AND AVOCADO WRAP

PREPARATION TIME: 10 min

COOKING TIME: 5 min

MODE OF COOKING: No Cook (only heating turkey)

SERVINGS: 2

INGREDIENTS:

- 4 oz. cooked turkey breast, thinly sliced
- 1/2 avocado, sliced
- 1 tsp olive oil
- 1/2 tsp chili powder
- 1/4 tsp cumin
- Salt and pepper to taste
- 2 whole-grain tortillas
- 1/2 cup shredded lettuce
- 1 small tomato, diced
- 2 Tbsp Greek yogurt (optional)

PROCEDURE:

1. Heat the turkey slices in a pan over medium heat for 2-3 min. Sprinkle with chili powder, cumin, salt, and pepper while heating.
2. Lay out the whole-grain tortillas and spread a small amount of Greek yogurt if desired.
3. Add a layer of shredded lettuce, diced tomatoes, and avocado slices.
4. Top with the spiced turkey slices.
5. Fold the sides of the tortilla in, then roll it up tightly.
6. Slice the wrap in half and serve immediately.

TIPS:

- For added heat, sprinkle a few red pepper flakes on top of the avocado slices.
- Make ahead and store in foil for a quick grab-and-go lunch.

NUTRITIONAL VALUES: Calories: 340, Fat: 15g, Carbs: 28g, Protein: 24g, Sugar: 2g

EGG SALAD LETTUCE WRAPS

PREPARATION TIME: 10 min

COOKING TIME: 0 min

MODE OF COOKING: No Cook

SERVINGS: 2

INGREDIENTS:

- 4 hard-boiled eggs, chopped
- 2 Tbsp Greek yogurt
- 1 tsp Dijon mustard
- 1 Tbsp lemon juice
- 1 Tbsp chopped chives
- Salt and pepper to taste
- 4 large romaine lettuce leaves
- 1/4 avocado, sliced (optional)
- 1 small cucumber, thinly sliced

PROCEDURE:

1. In a bowl, mix the chopped hard-boiled eggs, Greek yogurt, Dijon mustard, lemon juice, chives, salt, and pepper until combined.

2. Lay out the romaine lettuce leaves and spoon the egg salad evenly onto each leaf.

3. Add a few slices of avocado and cucumber to each lettuce wrap.

4. Roll up the lettuce wraps and secure with toothpicks if needed. Serve immediately.

TIPS:

- For extra crunch, add a few diced radishes or a sprinkle of sunflower seeds.
- These wraps are great for a low-carb lunch option.

NUTRITIONAL VALUES: Calories: 260, Fat: 18g, Carbs: 6g, Protein: 20g, Sugar: 1g

HUMMUS VEGGIE WRAP WITH QUINOA

PREPARATION TIME: 10 min

COOKING TIME: 0 min (quinoa pre-cooked)

MODE OF COOKING: No Cook

SERVINGS: 2

INGREDIENTS:

- 1/2 cup cooked quinoa, cooled
- 4 Tbsp hummus
- 2 whole-grain tortillas
- 1 small cucumber, sliced thin
- 1/2 cup shredded carrots
- 1/4 cup roasted red peppers, sliced
- 1/4 cup baby spinach
- 1 Tbsp sunflower seeds
- Salt and pepper to taste

PROCEDURE:

1. Lay out the whole-grain tortillas and spread 2 Tbsp of hummus on each tortilla.

2. Evenly divide the quinoa between the two tortillas, spreading it over the hummus.

3. Add cucumber slices, shredded carrots, roasted red peppers, spinach, and sunflower seeds.

4. Season with a pinch of salt and pepper.

5. Roll the tortillas tightly and slice in half. Serve immediately or wrap in foil for later.

TIPS:

- Try adding a drizzle of balsamic glaze for extra flavor.
- Make sure the quinoa is fully cooled before assembling the wraps to avoid soggy tortillas.

NUTRITIONAL VALUES: Calories: 330, Fat: 12g, Carbs: 42g, Protein: 10g, Sugar: 4g

8.3 VEGETARIAN AND VEGAN LUNCH OPTIONS

ZESTY QUINOA AND BLACK BEAN SALAD

PREPARATION TIME: 15 min

COOKING TIME: 20 min

MODE OF COOKING: Boiling

SERVINGS: 4

INGREDIENTS:

- 1 cup quinoa
- 2 cups water
- 1 can (15 oz.) black beans, rinsed and drained
- 1 red bell pepper, diced
- 1/4 cup fresh cilantro, chopped
- 1 avocado, diced
- 1 lime, juiced
- 2 Tbsp extra virgin olive oil
- Salt and pepper to taste

PROCEDURE:

1. Rinse quinoa under cold water until water runs clear.
2. In a medium saucepan, bring 2 cups of water to a boil. Add quinoa, reduce heat to low, cover, and simmer for 15-20 minutes until water is absorbed.
3. Remove from heat and let sit for 5 minutes, then fluff with a fork.
4. In a large bowl, mix cooked quinoa, black beans, red bell pepper, and cilantro.
5. In a small bowl, whisk together lime juice, olive oil, salt, and pepper to create a dressing.
6. Pour the dressing over the quinoa mixture. Add diced avocado and gently toss to combine.

TIPS:

- For an extra protein boost, add chopped grilled tofu or tempeh.
- Can be served cold or at room temperature.

NUTRITIONAL VALUES: Calories: 285, Fat: 15g, Carbs: 34g, Protein: 8g, Sugar: 2g

CREAMY VEGAN BROCCOLI SOUP

PREPARATION TIME: 10 min

COOKING TIME: 20 min

MODE OF COOKING: Simmering

SERVINGS: 4

INGREDIENTS:

- 2 Tbsp coconut oil
- 1 onion, chopped
- 2 cloves garlic, minced
- 4 cups broccoli florets
- 3 cups vegetable broth
- 1 can (14 oz.) coconut milk
- Salt and pepper to taste
- Crushed red pepper flakes (optional)

PROCEDURE:

1. In a large pot, heat coconut oil over medium heat. Add onion and

garlic, sauté until onion is translucent.

2. Add broccoli florets and vegetable broth. Bring to a boil, then reduce heat and simmer until broccoli is tender, about 15 minutes.

3. Add coconut milk and continue to simmer for another 5 minutes.

4. Using an immersion blender, puree the soup until smooth. Season with salt, pepper, and red pepper flakes if desired.

5. Serve hot.

TIPS:

- Top with a swirl of coconut cream and a sprinkle of toasted pumpkin seeds for extra flavor and crunch.

- Easily made in advance and reheated for a quick and nutritious meal.

NUTRITIONAL VALUES: Calories: 210, Fat: 16g, Carbs: 14g, Protein: 4g, Sugar: 5g

---

GRILLED VEGETABLE AND HUMMUS WRAP

PREPARATION TIME: 15 min

COOKING TIME: 10 min

MODE OF COOKING: Grilling

SERVINGS: 4

INGREDIENTS:

- 4 whole grain tortillas

- 1 zucchini, sliced lengthwise

- 1 yellow squash, sliced lengthwise

- 1 red onion, sliced into rings

- 1 red bell pepper, seeded and quartered

- 1 cup hummus

- 2 Tbsp olive oil

- Salt and pepper to taste

PROCEDURE:

1. Preheat grill to medium-high heat.

2. Brush zucchini, yellow squash, red onion, and bell pepper with olive oil and season with salt and pepper.

3. Grill vegetables until tender and charred, about 3-5 minutes per side.

4. Spread each tortilla with a layer of hummus. Top with grilled vegetables. Roll up tightly.

5. Cut each wrap in half and serve.

TIPS:

- Add fresh spinach or arugula for extra greens.

- For a gluten-free option, use gluten-free tortillas.

NUTRITIONAL VALUES: Calories: 290, Fat: 15g, Carbs: 34g, Protein: 9g, Sugar: 6g

CHAPTER 9: SATISFYING DINNERS TO FUEL YOUR EVENINGS

9.1 LEAN PROTEINS WITH VEGGIE SIDES FOR BALANCED NUTRITION

GRILLED SALMON WITH ASPARAGUS AND QUINOA

PREPARATION TIME: 15 min

COOKING TIME: 25 min

MODE OF COOKING: Grilling

SERVINGS: 4

INGREDIENTS:

- 4 salmon fillets, about 6 oz each
- 1 Tbsp olive oil
- Salt and pepper, to taste
- 1 bunch asparagus, ends trimmed
- 1 cup quinoa
- 2 cups water
- 1 lemon, halved for juice
- 1 garlic clove, minced
- 2 Tbsp fresh parsley, chopped

PROCEDURE:

1. Rinse quinoa under cold water and drain.
2. In a saucepan, bring 2 cups of water to a boil, add quinoa, reduce the heat to low, cover, and simmer for 15 min or until the water is absorbed.
3. While the quinoa cooks, preheat the grill to medium-high heat.
4. Brush salmon fillets and asparagus with olive oil, and season with salt and pepper.
5. Grill salmon, skin side down, for about 6-7 min on each side or until cooked through. Grill the asparagus alongside, turning occasionally, until tender and charred, about 5-7 min.
6. In a small bowl, mix lemon juice, garlic, and parsley.
7. Fluff quinoa with a fork, stir in half of the lemon mixture, and divide among plates.
8. Place grilled salmon and asparagus on top of quinoa, and drizzle with the remaining lemon mixture.

TIPS:

- Ensure your grill is hot before adding the salmon to prevent sticking.
- Keep a close eye on the asparagus as they can char quickly.

NUTRITIONAL VALUES: Calories: 410, Fat: 20g, Carbs: 30g, Protein: 35g, Sugar: 3g

TURKEY AND VEGGIE STIR-FRY

PREPARATION TIME: 20 min

COOKING TIME: 15 min

MODE OF COOKING: Stir-frying

SERVINGS: 4

INGREDIENTS:

- 1 lb ground turkey, lean
- 1 Tbsp coconut oil
- 1 onion, chopped
- 2 carrots, sliced
- 1 bell pepper, julienned
- 2 cups broccoli florets
- 2 Tbsp soy sauce (low sodium)
- 1 Tbsp ginger, minced
- 2 garlic cloves, minced
- 1 tsp sesame seeds for garnish
- 1 tsp red pepper flakes (optional)

PROCEDURE:

1. Heat coconut oil in a large skillet or wok over medium-high heat.
2. Add ground turkey and cook until browned, breaking it up as it cooks, about 5 min.
3. Add onion, carrots, bell pepper, and broccoli to the skillet. Stir-fry for about 7-8 min until vegetables are tender-crisp.
4. Add ginger, garlic, and soy sauce.

Cook, stirring frequently, for an additional 2 min.

5. Sprinkle with sesame seeds and red pepper flakes, if using.

TIPS:

- Add water or vegetable broth if the mixture seems dry during cooking.
- Serve with a side of brown rice or whole grain noodles to make it a more filling meal.

NUTRITIONAL VALUES: Calories: 295, Fat: 13g, Carbs: 15g, Protein: 28g, Sugar: 5g

HERB-ROASTED CHICKEN WITH ZUCCHINI AND TOMATOES

PREPARATION TIME: 20 min

COOKING TIME: 50 min

MODE OF COOKING: Roasting

SERVINGS: 4

INGREDIENTS:

- 4 skinless, boneless chicken breasts
- 2 Tbsp extra virgin olive oil

- 2 tsp dried Italian herbs
- Salt and pepper, to taste
- 3 zucchinis, sliced
- 1 cup cherry tomatoes, halved
- 3 cloves garlic, minced

PROCEDURE:

1. Preheat oven to 375°F (190°C).
2. Place chicken breasts in a baking dish. Drizzle with 1 Tbsp olive oil and rub with Italian herbs, garlic, salt, and pepper.
3. In a separate bowl, toss zucchini and tomatoes with the remaining olive oil and a pinch of salt and pepper.
4. Arrange the vegetables around the chicken in the baking dish.
5. Roast in the preheated oven for 50 min, or until the chicken is cooked through and vegetables are tender.

TIPS:

- Use parchment paper in the baking dish for easier cleaning.
- Squeeze a bit of fresh lemon over the chicken and veggies after roasting for extra zest.

NUTRITIONAL VALUES: Calories: 320, Fat: 14g, Carbs: 12g, Protein: 38g, Sugar: 4g

---

BAKED COD WITH ROASTED BRUSSELS SPROUTS AND SWEET POTATOES

PREPARATION TIME: 15 min

COOKING TIME: 25 min

MODE OF COOKING: Baking

SERVINGS: 2

INGREDIENTS:

- 2 cod fillets (about 4 oz. each)
- 1 Tbsp olive oil
- 1 tsp lemon zest
- 1 tsp garlic powder
- Salt and pepper to taste
- 1/2 lb Brussels sprouts, halved
- 1 medium sweet potato, cubed
- 1 Tbsp balsamic vinegar

PROCEDURE:

1. Preheat the oven to 400°F (200°C).
2. Toss the Brussels sprouts and sweet potato cubes with 1/2 Tbsp olive oil, balsamic vinegar, salt, and pepper. Spread them on a baking sheet.
3. Roast the vegetables in the oven for 20-25 min, turning halfway through.
4. While the veggies roast, season the cod fillets with olive oil, garlic powder, lemon zest, salt, and pepper.
5. Place the cod on a separate baking sheet and bake in the

oven for 10-12 min, until the fish is opaque and flakes easily with a fork.

6. Serve the baked cod alongside the roasted Brussels sprouts and sweet potatoes.

TIPS:

- Squeeze fresh lemon juice over the cod for extra flavor.
- Add a sprinkle of crushed red pepper to the roasted veggies for a bit of heat.

NUTRITIONAL VALUES: Calories: 400, Fat: 12g, Carbs: 45g, Protein: 30g, Sugar: 9g

---

LENTIL AND VEGGIE STEW WITH BROWN RICE

PREPARATION TIME: 10 min

COOKING TIME: 35 min

MODE OF COOKING: Simmering

SERVINGS: 4

INGREDIENTS:

- 1 cup dried lentils, rinsed
- 4 cups vegetable broth
- 1 onion, diced
- 2 cloves garlic, minced
- 1 carrot, diced
- 1 zucchini, diced
- 1 can (14.5 oz) diced tomatoes
- 1 tsp cumin
- 1/2 tsp smoked paprika
- Salt and pepper to taste
- 1 cup cooked brown rice

PROCEDURE:

1. In a large pot, sauté the onion and garlic over medium heat until softened (about 5 min).

2. Add the carrot, zucchini, cumin, smoked paprika, salt, and pepper, cooking for another 3-4 min.

3. Stir in the lentils, diced tomatoes, and vegetable broth. Bring to a boil, then reduce heat and simmer for 25-30 min until the lentils are tender.

4. Serve the stew over a bed of cooked brown rice.

TIPS:

- Add spinach during the last 5 min of cooking for extra greens.
- Use a pinch of chili powder for a spicier stew.

NUTRITIONAL VALUES: Calories: 320, Fat: 4g, Carbs: 55g, Protein: 15g, Sugar: 6g

---

GRILLED TOFU WITH SAUTÉED KALE AND QUINOA

PREPARATION TIME: 10 min

COOKING TIME: 20 min

MODE OF COOKING: Grilling and Sautéing

SERVINGS: 2

INGREDIENTS:

- 1 block (8 oz) extra-firm tofu, drained and pressed
- 1 Tbsp soy sauce (low sodium)
- 1 Tbsp olive oil
- 1 tsp garlic powder
- 2 cups kale, chopped
- 1 cup cooked quinoa
- 1 Tbsp lemon juice
- Salt and pepper to taste

PROCEDURE:

1. Preheat the grill to medium-high heat (about 375°F or 190°C).
2. Slice the tofu into 1/2-inch thick slabs and brush with olive oil, soy sauce, and garlic powder.
3. Grill the tofu for 4-5 min on each side until golden and slightly crisp.
4. In a pan, sauté the chopped kale with olive oil, salt, and pepper for 3-4 min until wilted.
5. Serve the grilled tofu over a bed of quinoa, topped with sautéed kale and a drizzle of lemon juice.

TIPS:

- Marinate the tofu for 15 min before grilling for extra flavor.
- Add a sprinkle of toasted sesame seeds on top for a nutty crunch.

NUTRITIONAL VALUES: Calories: 350, Fat: 15g, Carbs: 32g, Protein: 20g, Sugar: 3g

9.2 ONE-PAN MEALS FOR QUICK, HEALTHY DINNERS

LEMON GARLIC SALMON WITH ASPARAGUS

PREPARATION TIME: 10 min

COOKING TIME: 20 min

MODE OF COOKING: Sautéing

SERVINGS: 4

INGREDIENTS:

- 4 salmon fillets (6 oz. each)
- 1 lb. fresh asparagus, ends trimmed
- 2 Tbsp extra virgin olive oil
- 4 cloves garlic, minced
- 1 lemon, juiced and zested
- Salt and pepper to taste
- Fresh parsley, chopped (for garnish)

DIRECTIONS:

1. Heat olive oil in a large pan over medium-high heat.
2. Season the salmon with salt and pepper, then add to the pan, skin-side up. Cook for about 4-5 minutes on each side or until golden and cooked through.
3. Remove salmon and set aside.
4. In the same pan, add the minced

garlic and asparagus. Sauté for about 3-4 minutes.

5. Add lemon juice and zest, then stir to combine.

6. Return the salmon to the pan, cover, and let simmer for another 2-3 minutes.

7. Garnish with freshly chopped parsley before serving.

TIPS:

- Ensure not to overcook the salmon to keep it moist and tender.
- Serve with a side of quinoa or a fresh garden salad for a complete meal.

NUTRITIONAL VALUES: Calories: 300, Fat: 18g, Carbs: 8g, Protein: 29g, Sugar: 2g

---

CHICKEN AND VEGGIE SHEET PAN DINNER

PREPARATION TIME: 15 min

COOKING TIME: 25 min

MODE OF COOKING: Roasting

SERVINGS: 4

INGREDIENTS:

- 4 skinless, boneless chicken breasts
- 1 red bell pepper, sliced
- 1 yellow bell pepper, sliced
- 1 zucchini, sliced
- 1 red onion, sliced
- 2 Tbsp extra virgin olive oil
- 1 tsp dried oregano
- 1 tsp dried basil
- Salt and pepper to taste

DIRECTIONS:

1. Preheat oven to 425°F (220°C).

2. Place chicken and vegetables on a large baking sheet.

3. Drizzle with olive oil and sprinkle with oregano, basil, salt, and pepper.

4. Toss to coat evenly and spread out in a single layer.

5. Roast in the preheated oven for about 25 minutes, or until the chicken is cooked through and vegetables are tender.

6. Serve hot, garnished with fresh herbs if desired.

TIPS:

- Use parchment paper on the sheet pan for easy cleanup.
- Experiment with different vegetables like Brussels sprouts or carrots to suit your taste.

NUTRITIONAL VALUES: Calories: 250, Fat: 9g, Carbs: 12g, Protein: 28g, Sugar: 5g

ONE-PAN TURMERIC TOFU & CHICKPEAS

PREPARATION TIME: 10 min

COOKING TIME: 20 min

MODE OF COOKING: Sautéing

SERVINGS: 4

INGREDIENTS:

- 1 block tofu, pressed and cubed
- 1 can (15 oz.) chickpeas, drained and rinsed
- 1 large onion, sliced
- 2 Tbsp coconut oil
- 1 tsp turmeric
- 1 tsp cumin
- 1/2 tsp chili powder
- Salt and pepper to taste
- Fresh cilantro, chopped (for garnish)

DIRECTIONS:

1. Heat coconut oil in a large pan over medium heat.
2. Add onion and sauté until translucent.
3. Add tofu and chickpeas to the pan. Sprinkle with turmeric, cumin, chili powder, salt, and pepper.
4. Cook for about 10-15 minutes, stirring occasionally, until tofu is golden and chickpeas are slightly crispy.
5. Garnish with fresh cilantro before serving.

TIPS:

- Pressing the tofu for at least 30 minutes before cooking will help it absorb more flavor and improve its texture.
- Great served with a side of brown rice or naan bread.

NUTRITIONAL VALUES: Calories: 290, Fat: 15g, Carbs: 23g, Protein: 19g, Sugar: 4g

SPICY SHRIMP AND BROCCOLI STIR-FRY

PREPARATION TIME: 15 min

COOKING TIME: 10 min

MODE OF COOKING: Stir-Frying

SERVINGS: 4

INGREDIENTS:

- 1 lb. shrimp, peeled and deveined
- 1 head of broccoli, cut into florets
- 2 Tbsp sesame oil
- 3 cloves garlic, minced
- 1 Tbsp ginger, minced
- 2 Tbsp low-sodium soy sauce
- 1 Tbsp chili sauce
- 1 tsp honey
- Sesame seeds (for garnish)

DIRECTIONS:

1. Heat sesame oil in a large skillet over medium-high heat.
2. Add garlic and ginger, and sauté until fragrant.
3. Add broccoli and stir-fry for about

5 minutes, until it starts to soften.

4. Add the shrimp, soy sauce, chili sauce, and honey. Cook for another 5 minutes, or until shrimp are pink and fully cooked.

5. Serve hot, sprinkled with sesame seeds.

TIPS:

- Ensure not to overcook the shrimp to avoid a rubbery texture.
- Adjust the amount of chili sauce according to your spice preference.

NUTRITIONAL VALUES: Calories: 230, Fat: 10g, Carbs: 12g, Protein: 24g, Sugar: 3g

---

ONE-POT MEDITERRANEAN CHICKEN

PREPARATION TIME: 15 min

COOKING TIME: 30 min

MODE OF COOKING: Simmering

SERVINGS: 4

INGREDIENTS:

- 4 skinless, boneless chicken thighs
- 1 can (14 oz.) diced tomatoes
- 1 can (15 oz.) artichoke hearts, drained and quartered
- 1/2 cup Kalamata olives, pitted and halved
- 3 cloves garlic, minced
- 2 Tbsp olive oil
- 1 tsp dried basil
- 1 tsp dried oregano
- Salt and pepper to taste
- Feta cheese, crumbled (for garnish)

DIRECTIONS:

1. Heat olive oil in a large pot over medium heat.

2. Brown the chicken thighs on both sides, about 3-4 minutes per side.

3. Add garlic and sauté until fragrant.

4. Stir in tomatoes, artichoke hearts, olives, basil, oregano, salt, and pepper.

5. Bring to a simmer, cover, and cook for about 20 minutes, or until chicken is cooked through.

6. Garnish with feta cheese before serving.

TIPS:

- Serve with a side of quinoa or whole grain bread to soak up the delicious sauce.
- Add a splash of white wine to the sauce for extra flavor, if desired.

NUTRITIONAL VALUES: Calories: 290, Fat: 18g, Carbs: 13g, Protein: 22g, Sugar: 5g

CHAPTER 10: HEALTHY SNACKS AND SMALL MEALS

10.1 SNACKABLE SUPERFOODS FOR ENERGY AND FOCUS

ALMOND AND CHIA ENERGY BALLS

PREPARATION TIME: 15 min

COOKING TIME: 0 min (No cooking required)

MODE OF COOKING: None

SERVINGS: 10 balls

INGREDIENTS:

- 1/2 cup raw almonds
- 1/4 cup chia seeds
- 1/4 cup flaxseeds, ground
- 1/2 cup Medjool dates, pitted and chopped
- 2 Tbsp coconut oil
- 1 tsp vanilla extract

DIRECTIONS:

1. Place almonds in a food processor and pulse until they are finely chopped.
2. Add chia seeds, ground flaxseeds, chopped dates, coconut oil, and vanilla extract to the processor.
3. Pulse the mixture until it forms a sticky dough-like consistency.
4. Scoop out the mixture and form into 1-inch balls using your hands.
5. Place the balls on a baking sheet lined with parchment paper and refrigerate for at least 1 hour to set.

TIPS:

- Store energy balls in an airtight container in the refrigerator for up to a week or freeze for longer storage.
- You can roll these balls in unsweetened cocoa powder or crushed nuts for an extra flavor layer.

NUTRITIONAL VALUES: Calories: 120, Fat: 8g, Carbs: 10g, Protein: 3g, Sugar: 6g

KALE CHIPS WITH NUTRITIONAL YEAST

PREPARATION TIME: 10 min

COOKING TIME: 15 min

MODE OF COOKING: Baking

SERVINGS: 4

INGREDIENTS:

- 1 bunch kale, washed, dried, and torn into bite-sized pieces
- 2 Tbsp extra virgin olive oil
- 2 Tbsp nutritional yeast
- 1/2 tsp salt
- 1/4 tsp garlic powder

DIRECTIONS:

1. Preheat oven to 300°F (150°C).
2. In a large bowl, toss kale pieces with olive oil, nutritional yeast, salt, and garlic powder until fully coated.
3. Spread kale in a single layer on a baking sheet.
4. Bake for 15 minutes or until crisp, being careful not to burn.
5. Let chips cool for a few minutes before serving.

TIPS:

- Make sure kale leaves are thoroughly dry to ensure they become crispy.
- Custom tailor flavors by adding spices like smoked paprika or chili powder.

NUTRITIONAL VALUES: Calories: 80, Fat: 5g, Carbs: 7g, Protein: 4g, Sugar: 1g

---

POMEGRANATE QUINOA SALAD

PREPARATION TIME: 10 min

COOKING TIME: 15 min

MODE OF COOKING: Boiling

SERVINGS: 2

INGREDIENTS:

- 1 cup cooked quinoa
- 1/2 cup pomegranate seeds
- 1/4 cup diced cucumber
- 1/4 cup chopped almonds
- 2 Tbsp chopped fresh mint
- Juice of one lemon
- 2 Tbsp extra virgin olive oil
- Salt and pepper to taste

DIRECTIONS:

1. In a large bowl, mix cooked quinoa, pomegranate seeds, cucumber, almonds, and fresh mint.
2. In a small bowl, whisk together lemon juice, olive oil, salt, and pepper.
3. Pour dressing over the quinoa mixture and toss until everything is well coated.
4. Chill in the refrigerator for at least 30 minutes before serving to enhance flavors.

TIPS:

- Serve chilled as a refreshing, light snack or as a side with your favorite protein.

- Add arugula or spinach for added greenery and nutrition.

NUTRITIONAL VALUES: Calories: 220, Fat: 14g, Carbs: 23g, Protein: 6g, Sugar: 6g

GREEK YOGURT AND BERRY PARFAIT

PREPARATION TIME: 5 min

COOKING TIME: 0 min

MODE OF COOKING: No Cook

SERVINGS: 1

INGREDIENTS:

- 1/2 cup non-fat Greek yogurt
- 1/4 cup fresh blueberries
- 1/4 cup fresh strawberries, sliced
- 1 Tbsp chia seeds
- 1 Tbsp chopped walnuts
- 1 tsp honey (optional)

PROCEDURE:

1. In a small glass or bowl, layer half of the Greek yogurt at the bottom.
2. Add half of the blueberries and strawberries on top of the yogurt.
3. Sprinkle with half of the chia seeds and walnuts.
4. Repeat the layering with the remaining yogurt, berries, chia seeds, and walnuts.
5. Drizzle honey on top if desired and serve immediately.

TIPS:

- For added crunch, top with a tablespoon of granola.
- Make ahead and refrigerate for a quick grab-and-go snack.

NUTRITIONAL VALUES: Calories: 220, Fat: 9g, Carbs: 25g, Protein: 12g, Sugar: 10g

AVOCADO AND EGG TOAST

PREPARATION TIME: 5 min

COOKING TIME: 5 min

MODE OF COOKING: Toasting and Boiling

SERVINGS: 1

INGREDIENTS:

- 1 slice whole-grain bread
- 1/2 ripe avocado
- 1 hard-boiled egg, sliced
- Salt and pepper to taste
- 1/4 tsp red pepper flakes (optional)

PROCEDURE:

1. Toast the whole-grain bread to your liking.
2. While the bread is toasting, peel and slice the hard-boiled egg.
3. Mash the avocado and spread it evenly over the toasted bread.
4. Top with the sliced egg, and season with salt, pepper, and red pepper flakes if desired.

TIPS:

- For a protein boost, add a few slices of smoked salmon on top of the egg.
- Squeeze fresh lemon juice over the avocado for a tangy twist.

NUTRITIONAL VALUES: Calories: 250, Fat: 15g, Carbs: 20g, Protein: 10g, Sugar: 2g

ROASTED CHICKPEAS WITH PAPRIKA

PREPARATION TIME: 5 min

COOKING TIME: 30 min

MODE OF COOKING: Roasting

SERVINGS: 4

INGREDIENTS:

- 1 can (15 oz) chickpeas, drained and rinsed
- 1 Tbsp olive oil
- 1 tsp smoked paprika
- 1/2 tsp garlic powder
- Salt and pepper to taste

PROCEDURE:

1. Preheat the oven to 400°F (200°C).
2. Pat the chickpeas dry with a paper towel to remove excess moisture.
3. Toss the chickpeas with olive oil, smoked paprika, garlic powder, salt, and pepper.
4. Spread the chickpeas in a single layer on a baking sheet.
5. Roast for 25-30 min, stirring halfway through, until the chickpeas are crispy and golden brown.
6. Let them cool slightly before serving.

TIPS:

- Store in an airtight container for up to 3 days for a crunchy snack.
- Try adding different seasonings like cumin or chili powder for a flavor variation.

NUTRITIONAL VALUES: Calories: 180, Fat: 7g, Carbs: 25g, Protein: 7g, Sugar: 2g

10.2 Low-Carb and High-Protein Snack Recipes

<table>
<tr><td colspan="2" align="center">SMOKED SALMON AND AVOCADO ROLL-UPS</td></tr>
</table>

PREPARATION TIME: 10 min

COOKING TIME: 0 min

MODE OF COOKING: No cook

SERVINGS: 4

INGREDIENTS:

- 8 slices of smoked salmon
- 1 ripe avocado, thinly sliced
- 1/2 cucumber, julienned
- 1 Tbsp lemon juice
- 1/4 tsp black pepper
- 1 Tbsp chopped dill

DIRECTIONS:

1. Lay out the smoked salmon slices on a flat surface.
2. Arrange a few slices of avocado and some julienned cucumber on each salmon slice.
3. Sprinkle lemon juice and black pepper evenly across the salmon slices.
4. Carefully roll up the salmon slices, securing the fillings inside.
5. Garnish with chopped dill before serving.

TIPS:

- For a dairy-free creamy texture, blend the avocado with lemon juice before spreading on the salmon.
- Serve with a side of mixed greens for a complete snack.

NUTRITIONAL VALUES: Calories: 120, Fat: 9g, Carbs: 4g, Protein: 8g, Sugar: 1g

<table>
<tr><td colspan="2" align="center">ALMOND BUTTER AND BERRY ENERGY BALLS</td></tr>
</table>

PREPARATION TIME: 15 min

COOKING TIME: 0 min

MODE OF COOKING: No cook

SERVINGS: 10 balls

INGREDIENTS:

- 1/2 cup rolled oats
- 1/3 cup almond butter
- 1/4 cup flaxseeds, ground
- 1/4 cup honey
- 1/4 cup dried cranberries, chopped
- 2 Tbsp chia seeds

DIRECTIONS:

1. In a medium bowl, combine rolled oats, almond butter, ground flaxseeds, honey, chopped dried cranberries, and chia seeds.
2. Stir the mixture until well combined.
3. Using clean hands, roll the mixture into small balls, each about the size of a walnut.
4. Place the energy balls on a plate

and refrigerate for at least 30 min before serving to allow them to set.

TIPS:

- Keep energy balls refrigerated in an airtight container to maintain freshness.
- Substitute dried cranberries with chopped dried blueberries for variation.

NUTRITIONAL VALUES: Calories: 130, Fat: 7g, Carbs: 15g, Protein: 3g, Sugar: 9g

TOFU AND VEGGIE MINI FRITTATAS

PREPARATION TIME: 15 min
COOKING TIME: 25 min
MODE OF COOKING: Baking
SERVINGS: 6 mini frittatas
INGREDIENTS:

- 300g firm tofu, crumbled
- 1 Tbsp olive oil
- 1/2 cup diced bell peppers
- 1/4 cup chopped spinach
- 1/4 tsp turmeric
- 1/4 tsp salt
- 1/4 tsp black pepper

DIRECTIONS:

1. Preheat oven to 375°F (190°C) and grease a 6-cup muffin tin.
2. Heat olive oil in a skillet over medium heat and sauté bell peppers until soft.
3. In a large bowl, combine crumbled tofu, cooked bell peppers, chopped spinach, turmeric, salt, and black pepper.
4. Spoon the mixture into the muffin tins, pressing lightly to compact.
5. Bake for 25 min or until the frittatas are firm and lightly golden on top.
6. Let cool for 5 min before removing from the tin and serving.

TIPS:

- Add a pinch of nutritional yeast for a cheesy flavor without the dairy.
- These frittatas can be stored in the refrigerator for up to 5 days.

NUTRITIONAL VALUES: Calories: 100, Fat: 6g, Carbs: 4g, Protein: 8g, Sugar: 1g

SPICED CHICKPEA CRUNCHIES

PREPARATION TIME: 10 min
COOKING TIME: 30 min
MODE OF COOKING: Roasting
SERVINGS: 4
INGREDIENTS:

- 1 can (15 oz.) chickpeas, rinsed and drained

- 1 Tbsp olive oil
- 1/2 tsp ground cumin
- 1/4 tsp chili powder
- 1/4 tsp salt

DIRECTIONS:

1. Preheat oven to 400°F (204°C).
2. Pat chickpeas dry with paper towels, removing as much moisture as possible.
3. Toss dry chickpeas with olive oil, cumin, chili powder, and salt.
4. Spread the chickpeas on a baking sheet in a single layer.
5. Roast for 30 min, shaking the pan halfway through for even cooking.
6. Remove from oven when chickpeas are crunchy and allow to cool before serving.

TIPS:

- Enjoy as a snack on their own or toss into salads for a protein boost.
- Store in an airtight container at room temperature to maintain crunch.

NUTRITIONAL VALUES: Calories: 120, Fat: 5g, Carbs: 15g, Protein: 5g, Sugar: 0g

GREEK YOGURT WITH MIXED NUTS AND SEEDS

PREPARATION TIME: 5 min

COOKING TIME: 0 min

MODE OF COOKING: Mixing

SERVINGS: 1

INGREDIENTS:

- 1 cup non-fat Greek yogurt
- 1 Tbsp chopped almonds
- 1 Tbsp walnuts, chopped
- 1 Tbsp pumpkin seeds
- 1 tsp honey (optional)

DIRECTIONS:

1. In a serving bowl, combine Greek yogurt with chopped almonds, walnuts, and pumpkin seeds.
2. Drizzle with honey if desired, for a touch of sweetness.
3. Stir to mix well before serving.

TIPS:

- Customize by adding a sprinkle of cinnamon or a few fresh berries for extra flavor and nutrition.

NUTRITIONAL VALUES: Calories: 220, Fat: 12g, Carbs: 10g, Protein: 20g, Sugar: 9g

10.3 EASY-TO-PREPARE SNACKS FOR BUSY DAYS

ALMOND BUTTER & BERRY RICE CAKES

PREPARATION TIME: 5 min.

COOKING TIME: 0 min.

MODE OF COOKING: No cooking required

SERVINGS: 2

INGREDIENTS:

- 2 whole-grain rice cakes
- 2 Tbsp almond butter (smooth)
- 1/2 cup fresh blueberries
- 1/2 cup fresh raspberries
- 1 Tbsp chia seeds

DIRECTIONS:

1. Spread 1 tablespoon of almond butter evenly on each rice cake.
2. Top each rice cake with an equal amount of blueberries and raspberries.
3. Sprinkle chia seeds over the top of the berries.

TIPS:

- For extra freshness, add a few mint leaves before serving.
- If berries are out of season, substitute with thinly sliced apple or pear.

NUTRITIONAL VALUES: Calories: 180, Fat: 9g, Carbs: 22g, Protein: 4g, Sugar: 6g

TUNA-STUFFED AVOCADO BOATS

PREPARATION TIME: 10 min.

COOKING TIME: 0 min.

MODE OF COOKING: No cooking required

SERVINGS: 2

INGREDIENTS:

- 1 large ripe avocado, halved and pitted
- 1 can (5 oz.) tuna in water, drained and flaked
- 1/4 cup diced red bell pepper
- 2 Tbsp chopped red onion
- 1 Tbsp lemon juice
- Salt and pepper to taste
- Fresh cilantro for garnish

DIRECTIONS:

1. Scoop out some of the avocado flesh to create a larger cavity, and chop the removed avocado.
2. In a bowl, mix the flaked tuna, diced bell pepper, chopped onion, lemon juice, and the chopped

avocado.

3. Season the mixture with salt and pepper.
4. Spoon the tuna mixture back into the avocado halves.
5. Garnish with fresh cilantro before serving.

TIPS:

- Serve with a fresh green salad to round out the meal.
- Drizzle with a little olive oil for an extra healthy fat boost.

NUTRITIONAL VALUES: Calories: 300, Fat: 22g, Carbs: 12g, Protein: 15g, Sugar: 2g

QUICK COTTAGE CHEESE AND PINEAPPLE BOWL

PREPARATION TIME: 5 min.

COOKING TIME: 0 min.

MODE OF COOKING: No cooking required

SERVINGS: 1

INGREDIENTS:

- 1 cup non-fat cottage cheese
- 1/2 cup chopped fresh pineapple
- 1 Tbsp flaxseeds

DIRECTIONS:

1. Place the cottage cheese in a serving bowl.
2. Top with chopped pineapple.
3. Sprinkle flaxseeds over the top.

TIPS:

- For added sweetness and crunch, sprinkle a few crushed walnuts on top.
- Swap pineapple for any other fresh fruit like berries or mango for variety.

NUTRITIONAL VALUES: Calories: 200, Fat: 3g, Carbs: 20g, Protein: 20g, Sugar: 10g

MEDITERRANEAN VEGGIE HUMMUS WRAP

PREPARATION TIME: 10 min.

COOKING TIME: 0 min.

MODE OF COOKING: No cooking required

SERVINGS: 1

INGREDIENTS:

- 1 whole-grain wrap
- 3 Tbsp hummus
- 1/4 cup sliced cucumber
- 1/4 cup chopped tomatoes
- 1/4 cup shredded carrots
- 1/4 cup sliced red onions
- 2 Tbsp crumbled feta cheese
- 1 Tbsp balsamic vinegar

DIRECTIONS:

1. Spread the hummus evenly across the surface of the wrap.
2. Layer the cucumber, tomatoes, carrots, and red onions over the hummus.

3. Sprinkle feta cheese on top.

4. Drizzle with balsamic vinegar.

5. Roll up the wrap tightly and cut in half to serve.

TIPS:

- To add more protein, include a few slices of grilled chicken or turkey.

- For a vegan option, omit the feta or replace it with vegan cheese.

NUTRITIONAL VALUES: Calories: 290, Fat: 14g, Carbs: 34g, Protein: 10g, Sugar: 5g

CHAPTER 11: GUILT-FREE DESSERTS

11.1 LOW-SUGAR, HIGH-FLAVOR DESSERT IDEAS

CHIA BERRY PUDDING

PREPARATION TIME: 15 min

COOKING TIME: 0 min (rest in refrigerator for at least 3 hrs)

MODE OF COOKING: Refrigeration

SERVINGS: 2

INGREDIENTS:

- 1/4 cup chia seeds
- 1 cup unsweetened almond milk
- 1/2 tsp vanilla extract
- 1 Tbsp honey or maple syrup (optional)
- 1/2 cup mixed berries (blueberries, raspberries, strawberries), fresh or frozen
- Mint leaves for garnish (optional)

DIRECTIONS:

1. In a medium bowl, mix chia seeds, almond milk, vanilla extract, and honey (if using).
2. Stir the mixture well to combine and prevent any clumps.
3. Cover the bowl and refrigerate for at least 3 hours, allowing the chia seeds to swell and form a pudding-like texture.
4. Once set, stir the pudding again, and layer or top with mixed berries.
5. Garnish with mint leaves before serving, if desired.

TIPS:

- For a smoother consistency, blend the pudding with an immersion blender before refrigerating.
- Adjust sweetness according to taste, and use stevia as a lower-calorie sweetener if preferred.
- If using frozen berries, let them thaw slightly before adding to the pudding for enhanced flavor.

NUTRITIONAL VALUES: Calories: 150, Fat: 7g, Carbs: 18g, Protein: 4g, Sugar: 8g

AVOCADO CHOCOLATE MOUSSE

PREPARATION TIME: 10 min

COOKING TIME: 0 min

MODE OF COOKING: Blending

SERVINGS: 2

INGREDIENTS:

- 1 ripe avocado, peeled and pitted
- 2 Tbsp unsweetened cocoa powder
- 1/4 cup coconut milk
- 1 Tbsp honey or maple syrup (optional)

- 1/2 tsp vanilla extract

DIRECTIONS:

1. Place the avocado, cocoa powder, coconut milk, honey (if using), and vanilla extract in a blender.

2. Blend until smooth and creamy, scraping down the sides as necessary.

3. Transfer the mousse to serving dishes and refrigerate for at least 1 hour to set.

4. Serve chilled with a dusting of extra cocoa powder or some fresh berries on top.

TIPS:

- Ensure the avocado is fully ripe for best flavor and texture.

- For a vegan version, use maple syrup instead of honey.

- Can be stored in the refrigerator for up to 2 days, covered to prevent browning.

NUTRITIONAL VALUES: Calories: 230, Fat: 17g, Carbs: 19g, Protein: 3g, Sugar: 6g

---

COCONUT AND ALMOND FLOUR COOKIES

PREPARATION TIME: 10 min

COOKING TIME: 12 min

MODE OF COOKING: Baking

SERVINGS: 12 cookies

INGREDIENTS:

- 1 cup almond flour
- 1/2 cup unsweetened shredded coconut
- 1/4 cup coconut oil, melted
- 1 egg
- 1/4 cup honey or maple syrup
- 1/2 tsp vanilla extract
- 1/4 tsp baking soda
- Pinch of salt

PROCEDURE:

1. Preheat the oven to 350°F (175°C) and line a baking sheet with parchment paper.

2. In a medium bowl, mix almond flour, shredded coconut, baking soda, and salt.

3. In another bowl, whisk together the egg, coconut oil, honey, and vanilla extract.

4. Combine the wet and dry ingredients, mixing until a dough forms.

5. Scoop small spoonfuls of dough onto the prepared baking sheet and flatten slightly.

6. Bake for 10-12 minutes or until golden around the edges.

7. Let the cookies cool before serving.

TIPS:

- Store in an airtight container for

up to 5 days.

- Add dark chocolate chips for an extra treat.

NUTRITIONAL VALUES: Calories: 120, Fat: 9g, Carbs: 7g, Protein: 3g, Sugar: 4g

BAKED APPLES WITH CINNAMON AND WALNUTS

PREPARATION TIME: 10 min

COOKING TIME: 25 min

MODE OF COOKING: Baking

SERVINGS: 4

INGREDIENTS:

- 4 medium apples, cored
- 1/4 cup walnuts, chopped
- 2 Tbsp raisins
- 1 Tbsp honey
- 1 tsp ground cinnamon
- 1/2 tsp vanilla extract
- 1/4 cup water

PROCEDURE:

1. Preheat the oven to 350°F (175°C).
2. In a small bowl, mix chopped walnuts, raisins, honey, cinnamon, and vanilla extract.
3. Stuff the cored apples with the walnut mixture and place them in a baking dish.
4. Pour the water into the bottom of the dish and bake the apples for 25 minutes or until tender.
5. Let cool slightly before serving.

TIPS:

- Serve with a dollop of Greek yogurt for extra creaminess.
- Use pears as a substitute for apples for a different flavor.

NUTRITIONAL VALUES: Calories: 150, Fat: 5g, Carbs: 26g, Protein: 2g, Sugar: 20g

---

DARK CHOCOLATE AND AVOCADO TRUFFLES

PREPARATION TIME: 15 min

COOKING TIME: 0 min (Chill for 30 min)

MODE OF COOKING: No Cook

SERVINGS: 12 truffles

INGREDIENTS:

- 1 ripe avocado, mashed
- 1/2 cup dark chocolate (70% cocoa), melted
- 2 Tbsp unsweetened cocoa powder
- 1 tsp vanilla extract
- Pinch of sea salt

PROCEDURE:

1. In a medium bowl, mash the ripe avocado until smooth.
2. Stir in the melted dark chocolate, vanilla extract, and sea salt until fully combined.
3. Place the mixture in the refrigerator to chill for 30 minutes.
4. Once chilled, scoop small portions of the mixture and roll them into balls.
5. Roll each truffle in unsweetened cocoa powder to coat.
6. Keep the truffles chilled until ready to serve.

TIPS:

- Add a pinch of cayenne pepper for a spicy twist.
- Store in an airtight container in the fridge for up to 3 days.

NUTRITIONAL VALUES: Calories: 90, Fat: 7g, Carbs: 7g, Protein: 1g, Sugar: 2g

---

BANANA OATMEAL MUFFINS

PREPARATION TIME: 10 min

COOKING TIME: 20 min

MODE OF COOKING: Baking

SERVINGS: 8 muffins

INGREDIENTS:

- 2 ripe bananas, mashed
- 1 cup rolled oats
- 1/4 cup almond flour
- 1 egg
- 1/4 cup almond milk
- 1 Tbsp honey
- 1 tsp baking powder
- 1/2 tsp cinnamon
- Pinch of salt

PROCEDURE:

1. Preheat the oven to 350°F (175°C) and grease or line a muffin tin.
2. In a large bowl, mix mashed bananas, egg, almond milk, and honey.
3. In a separate bowl, combine oats, almond flour, baking powder, cinnamon, and salt.
4. Gradually add the dry ingredients to the wet ingredients, stirring until just combined.
5. Pour the batter evenly into the prepared muffin tin.
6. Bake for 18-20 minutes, or until a toothpick inserted comes out clean.
7. Let the muffins cool before serving.

TIPS:

- Add blueberries or chopped nuts to the batter for added texture.
- These muffins freeze well, making

them perfect for meal prep.

NUTRITIONAL VALUES: Calories: 130, Fat: 5g, Carbs: 18g, Protein: 3g, Sugar: 5g

11.2 HEALTHY TAKES ON TRADITIONAL SWEETS

ZESTY LEMON GREEK YOGURT CAKE

PREPARATION TIME: 20 min

COOKING TIME: 35 min

MODE OF COOKING: Baking

SERVINGS: 8

INGREDIENTS:

- 1 1/2 cups whole wheat flour
- 2 tsp baking powder
- 1/2 tsp salt
- 1 cup non-fat Greek yogurt
- 1 cup granulated erythritol (or equivalent sweetener)
- 3 large eggs
- 2 tsp grated lemon zest (approximately 2 lemons)
- 1/2 tsp pure vanilla extract
- 1/2 cup extra virgin olive oil
- 1/4 cup freshly squeezed lemon juice

DIRECTIONS:

1. Preheat oven to 350°F (177°C). Grease and flour a 9-inch cake pan or line it with parchment paper.
2. In a medium bowl, whisk together the whole wheat flour, baking powder, and salt.
3. In a large bowl, mix the Greek yogurt, erythritol, eggs, lemon zest, vanilla extract, and extra virgin olive oil until well combined.
4. Gradually add the dry ingredients to the wet mixture, stirring until just blended.
5. Incorporate the lemon juice, and stir gently to combine.
6. Pour the batter into the prepared cake pan and smooth the top with a spatula.
7. Bake for about 35 minutes, or until a toothpick inserted into the center of the cake comes out clean.
8. Let the cake cool in the pan for 10 minutes, then turn out onto a wire rack to cool completely.

TIPS:

- For extra lemon flavor, drizzle with a sugar-free lemon glaze made by mixing lemon juice with powdered erythritol.
- Serve with a dollop of whipped coconut cream for a luxurious touch.

NUTRITIONAL VALUES: Calories: 190, Fat: 10g, Carbs: 22g, Protein: 7g, Sugar: 3g

---

FLOURLESS CHOCOLATE WALNUT BROWNIES

PREPARATION TIME: 15 min

COOKING TIME: 25 min

MODE OF COOKING: Baking

SERVINGS: 12

INGREDIENTS:

- 1 cup pureed ripe avocado
- 1/2 cup unsweetened cocoa powder
- 1/2 cup almond flour
- 3/4 cup erythritol
- 2 eggs
- 1 tsp vanilla extract
- 1/2 tsp baking powder
- 1/4 tsp salt
- 1/2 cup chopped walnuts

DIRECTIONS:

1. Preheat oven to 350°F (177°C). Line an 8x8 inch baking pan with parchment paper.
2. In a mixing bowl, blend the pureed avocado, cocoa powder, and almond flour until smooth.
3. Add erythritol, eggs, vanilla extract, baking powder, and salt to the mixture and mix until thoroughly combined.
4. Fold in the chopped walnuts.
5. Spread the batter evenly into the prepared pan.
6. Bake for 25 minutes, or until the edges are set but the center is still slightly undercooked.
7. Let the brownies cool in the pan, then cut into squares.

TIPS:

- These brownies are best enjoyed when slightly undercooked to maintain a fudgy texture.
- Store in an airtight container in the refrigerator to keep them fresh.

NUTRITIONAL VALUES: Calories: 130, Fat: 9g, Carbs: 13g, Protein: 4g, Sugar: 1g

---

COCONUT FLOUR PANCAKES

PREPARATION TIME: 10 min

COOKING TIME: 10 min

MODE OF COOKING: Pan-frying

SERVINGS: 4 pancakes

INGREDIENTS:

- 1/4 cup coconut flour
- 2 large eggs
- 1/4 cup almond milk (unsweetened)
- 1 Tbsp coconut oil, melted
- 1/2 tsp baking powder
- 1 tsp vanilla extract

- Pinch of salt

PROCEDURE:

1. In a medium bowl, whisk together the eggs, almond milk, coconut oil, and vanilla extract.

2. Add coconut flour, baking powder, and salt to the wet ingredients, stirring until a smooth batter forms.

3. Heat a non-stick pan over medium heat and lightly grease with coconut oil.

4. Pour 1/4 cup of batter onto the pan and cook for 2-3 minutes per side until golden.

5. Repeat with the remaining batter and serve with fresh berries or a drizzle of honey.

TIPS:

- For extra flavor, add cinnamon or nutmeg to the batter.
- These pancakes freeze well for quick breakfasts during the week.

NUTRITIONAL VALUES: Calories: 130, Fat: 8g, Carbs: 7g, Protein: 6g, Sugar: 2g

HEALTHY BANANA BREAD

PREPARATION TIME: 10 min

COOKING TIME: 50 min

MODE OF COOKING: Baking

SERVINGS: 8 slices

INGREDIENTS:

- 2 ripe bananas, mashed
- 2 large eggs
- 1/4 cup Greek yogurt (non-fat)
- 1/4 cup honey or maple syrup
- 1 tsp vanilla extract
- 1 cup whole wheat flour
- 1/2 cup almond flour
- 1 tsp baking soda
- 1/2 tsp cinnamon
- Pinch of salt

PROCEDURE:

1. Preheat the oven to 350°F (175°C) and grease a loaf pan.

2. In a large bowl, combine mashed bananas, eggs, Greek yogurt, honey, and vanilla extract.

3. In a separate bowl, mix whole wheat flour, almond flour, baking soda, cinnamon, and salt.

4. Slowly add the dry ingredients to the wet mixture and stir until just combined.

5. Pour the batter into the greased loaf pan and bake for 45-50 minutes, or until a toothpick inserted into the center comes out clean.

6. Let the banana bread cool before slicing.

TIPS:

- Add walnuts or dark chocolate

chips to the batter for a bit of crunch or sweetness.

- This banana bread stays fresh for several days and can be frozen for later.

NUTRITIONAL VALUES: Calories: 180, Fat: 6g, Carbs: 28g, Protein: 5g, Sugar: 10g

OATMEAL RAISIN COOKIES

PREPARATION TIME: 10 min

COOKING TIME: 12 min

MODE OF COOKING: Baking

SERVINGS: 12 cookies

INGREDIENTS:

- 1 cup rolled oats
- 1/2 cup almond flour
- 1/4 cup coconut oil, melted
- 1/4 cup honey
- 1 egg
- 1 tsp vanilla extract
- 1/2 tsp cinnamon
- 1/4 cup raisins
- 1/4 tsp baking soda
- Pinch of salt

PROCEDURE:

1. Preheat the oven to 350°F (175°C) and line a baking sheet with parchment paper.
2. In a large bowl, combine rolled oats, almond flour, baking soda, cinnamon, and salt.

3. In another bowl, whisk together the melted coconut oil, honey, egg, and vanilla extract.
4. Pour the wet ingredients into the dry mixture and stir to combine.
5. Fold in the raisins.
6. Scoop small spoonfuls of dough onto the baking sheet and bake for 10-12 minutes, until golden.
7. Let the cookies cool before serving.

TIPS:

- Substitute the raisins with dried cranberries or dark chocolate chips for variety.
- Store in an airtight container for up to a week.

NUTRITIONAL VALUES: Calories: 110, Fat: 6g, Carbs: 14g, Protein: 2g, Sugar: 6g

PUMPKIN SPICE MUFFINS

PREPARATION TIME: 10 min

COOKING TIME: 20 min

MODE OF COOKING: Baking

SERVINGS: 8 muffins

INGREDIENTS:

- 1 cup almond flour
- 1/2 cup pumpkin puree
- 2 large eggs
- 1/4 cup honey or maple syrup
- 1 tsp vanilla extract

- 1 tsp pumpkin pie spice
- 1/2 tsp baking powder
- Pinch of salt

PROCEDURE:

1. Preheat the oven to 350°F (175°C) and line a muffin tin with liners.
2. In a large bowl, mix pumpkin puree, eggs, honey, and vanilla extract.
3. In a separate bowl, whisk almond flour, pumpkin pie spice, baking powder, and salt.
4. Combine the dry ingredients with the wet mixture, stirring until smooth.
5. Pour the batter into the muffin liners and bake for 18-20 minutes, or until a toothpick comes out clean.
6. Let the muffins cool before serving.

TIPS:

- Sprinkle chopped pecans on top of the batter before baking for added texture.
- These muffins make for a great fall treat or breakfast option.

NUTRITIONAL VALUES: Calories: 130, Fat: 7g, Carbs: 14g, Protein: 4g, Sugar: 7g

11.3 QUICK AND SIMPLE TREATS FOR CRAVINGS

NO-BAKE BERRY CASHEW CREAM BARS

PREPARATION TIME: 20 min

COOKING TIME: 0 min (Freezing Time: 4 hrs)

MODE OF COOKING: Freezing

SERVINGS: 8

INGREDIENTS:

- 1 cup raw cashews, soaked overnight
- 1 cup mixed berries (blueberries, raspberries, strawberries), fresh or frozen
- 1 ripe banana
- 1/4 cup coconut oil, melted
- 2 Tbsp honey or maple syrup (optional for sweetness)
- 1/2 tsp vanilla extract
- A pinch of salt

PROCEDURE:

1. Drain and rinse the soaked cashews thoroughly.
2. In a blender, combine cashews, mixed berries, banana, coconut oil, honey (if using), vanilla extract, and salt. Blend until smooth and creamy.
3. Line a small baking dish with parchment paper and pour the mixture into the dish, spreading evenly.
4. Freeze for at least 4 hours or until firm.
5. Remove from the freezer, let sit for a few minutes, then cut into bars.

TIPS:

- Keep bars stored in the freezer and allow a few minutes to soften before enjoying for optimal texture.
- Experiment with different berry combinations to find your favorite flavor profile.

NUTRITIONAL VALUES: Calories: 200, Fat: 15g, Carbs: 14g, Protein: 4g, Sugar: 7g

CINNAMON SPICED APPLE CHIPS

PREPARATION TIME: 10 min

COOKING TIME: 2 hrs

MODE OF COOKING: Baking

SERVINGS: 4

INGREDIENTS:

- 2 large apples, cored and thinly sliced
- 1 tsp ground cinnamon
- A sprinkle of nutmeg (optional)

PROCEDURE:

1. Preheat oven to 200°F (93°C).
2. Arrange apple slices in a single layer on a baking sheet lined with parchment paper.
3. Sprinkle evenly with cinnamon, and nutmeg if using.
4. Bake in the preheated oven for 1 hour, then flip slices and bake for another 1 hour or until crispy.
5. Remove from oven and allow to cool completely to crisp up further.

TIPS:

- Choose firm and slightly tart apples like Granny Smith for the best texture and flavor after baking.
- Ensure slices are of even thickness to promote uniform cooking.

NUTRITIONAL VALUES: Calories: 50, Fat: 0g, Carbs: 13g, Protein: 0g, Sugar: 10g

CHOCOLATE AVOCADO MOUSSE

PREPARATION TIME: 15 min

COOKING TIME: 0 min

MODE OF COOKING: Blending

SERVINGS: 4

INGREDIENTS:

- 2 ripe avocados, peeled and pitted
- 1/4 cup cocoa powder
- 1/4 cup honey or maple syrup
- 1 tsp vanilla extract
- 1/2 cup almond milk, unsweetened

PROCEDURE:

1. Place all ingredients in a blender.
2. Blend until smooth and creamy, scraping down the sides as necessary.
3. Spoon into serving dishes and refrigerate for at least 1 hour before serving.
4. Garnish with a sprinkle of cocoa powder or fresh berries if desired.

TIPS:

- For a richer flavor, add a pinch of sea salt or a spoonful of instant coffee powder.
- This mousse can also be used as

a frosting for cakes or cupcakes.

NUTRITIONAL VALUES: Calories: 240, Fat: 15g, Carbs: 28g, Protein: 3g, Sugar: 17g

FROZEN YOGURT BARK WITH NUTS AND BERRIES

PREPARATION TIME: 10 min

COOKING TIME: 0 min (Freezing Time: 3 hrs)

MODE OF COOKING: Freezing

SERVINGS: 6

INGREDIENTS:

- 2 cups non-fat Greek yogurt
- 1 Tbsp honey
- 1/2 tsp vanilla extract
- 1/4 cup sliced almonds
- 1/4 cup chopped walnuts
- 1/2 cup mixed berries (blueberries, raspberries)

PROCEDURE:

1. In a medium bowl, mix Greek yogurt with honey and vanilla extract.
2. Spread the yogurt mixture evenly on a baking sheet lined with parchment paper.
3. Sprinkle with sliced almonds, chopped walnuts, and berries.
4. Freeze until solid, about 3 hours.
5. Break into pieces and serve immediately.

TIPS:

- Mix in some chia or flax seeds for an added boost of omega-3 fatty acids.
- Keep the bark stored in the freezer in an airtight container for up to a month.

NUTRITIONAL VALUES: Calories: 130, Fat: 6g, Carbs: 10g, Protein: 9g, Sugar: 8g

---

PEANUT BUTTER BANANA ICE CREAM

PREPARATION TIME: 5 min

COOKING TIME: 0 min (Freezing Time: 2 hrs)

MODE OF COOKING: Blending

SERVINGS: 2

INGREDIENTS:

- 3 ripe bananas, sliced and frozen
- 2 Tbsp natural peanut butter

PROCEDURE:

1. Place frozen banana slices in a food processor or high-speed blender.
2. Pulse until they begin to break down, then add peanut butter.
3. Continue to blend until smooth, creamy, and resembles soft-serve ice cream.
4. Serve immediately or freeze for an additional hour for a firmer texture.

TIPS:

- Add a splash of almond milk for a creamier texture if needed.
- Sprinkle with dark chocolate chips or cocoa nibs for an extra treat.

NUTRITIONAL VALUES: Calories: 210, Fat: 8g, Carbs: 35g, Protein: 5g, Sugar: 18g

CHAPTER 12: MEAL PREP RECIPES FOR THE WEEK

12.1 BATCH COOKING TECHNIQUES FOR TIME EFFICIENCY

QUINOA CHICKEN VEGETABLE STEW

PREPARATION TIME: 20 min

COOKING TIME: 35 min

MODE OF COOKING: Simmering

SERVINGS: 6

INGREDIENTS:

- 1 lb skinless chicken breast, cubed
- 1 cup quinoa, rinsed
- 1 Tbsp extra virgin olive oil
- 3 cups low sodium chicken broth
- 1 onion, chopped
- 2 carrots, peeled and diced
- 2 celery stalks, diced
- 1 red bell pepper, chopped
- 1 zucchini, diced
- 3 cloves garlic, minced
- 1 tsp dried thyme
- 1 tsp dried basil
- Salt and black pepper to taste

DIRECTIONS:

1. Heat olive oil in a large pot over medium heat.
2. Add garlic and onion, sauté until onions are translucent.
3. Add chicken cubes to the pot, and cook until slightly browned.
4. Stir in carrots, celery, bell pepper, and zucchini, cook for 5 minutes.
5. Add quinoa, chicken broth, thyme, basil, salt, and pepper.
6. Bring to a boil, then reduce heat to low and simmer covered for 25 minutes until quinoa is cooked and vegetables are tender.

TIPS:

- For a vegetarian version, substitute chicken with chickpeas.
- Add a squeeze of lemon juice before serving for an extra zing.
- Serve hot with a side of whole-grain bread for additional fiber.

NUTRITIONAL VALUES: Calories: 310, Fat: 6g, Carbs: 38g, Protein: 28g, Sugar: 5g

SALMON AND KALE SWEET POTATO HASH

PREPARATION TIME: 15 min

COOKING TIME: 30 min

MODE OF COOKING: Pan-frying

SERVINGS: 4

INGREDIENTS:

- 2 medium sweet potatoes, peeled and diced
- 1 lb salmon, skin removed and cubed
- 2 cups kale, chopped

- 1 tbsp coconut oil
- 1 medium onion, diced
- 2 cloves garlic, minced
- Salt and black pepper to taste
- 1 tsp smoked paprika

DIRECTIONS:

1. Heat coconut oil in a large skillet over medium heat.
2. Add onion and garlic, sauté until onion becomes translucent.
3. Increase the heat to medium-high, add sweet potatoes and cook for 10 minutes until they start to soften.
4. Add salmon cubes, kale, smoked paprika, salt, and pepper.
5. Cook for another 10 minutes, stirring occasionally, until salmon is cooked through and sweet potatoes are tender.
6. Serve immediately.

TIPS:

- Add a dollop of non-fat Greek yogurt on top for extra creaminess.
- Perfect for a hearty breakfast or a nutritious dinner.

NUTRITIONAL VALUES: Calories: 400, Fat: 14g, Carbs: 34g, Protein: 35g, Sugar: 7g

LENTIL VEGGIE SOUP

PREPARATION TIME: 15 min

COOKING TIME: 45 min

MODE OF COOKING: Simmering

SERVINGS: 6

INGREDIENTS:

- 1 cup dried lentils, rinsed
- 1 Tbsp extra virgin olive oil
- 1 onion, diced
- 2 carrots, diced
- 2 stalks celery, diced
- 1 red bell pepper, diced
- 2 tomatoes, diced
- 6 cups vegetable broth
- 2 tsp dried oregano
- 1 tsp dried basil
- Salt and pepper to taste

DIRECTIONS:

1. Heat olive oil in a large pot over medium heat.
2. Add onion, carrots, celery, and bell pepper and sauté until onions are translucent and aromatic.
3. Stir in tomatoes and cook for

another 3 minutes.

4. Add lentils, broth, oregano, basil, salt, and pepper.

5. Bring to a boil, then reduce heat to low and let simmer for 35 minutes until lentils and vegetables are tender.

TIPS:

- Enhance the flavor with a handful of chopped fresh parsley before serving.

- This soup freezes well for quick future meals.

NUTRITIONAL VALUES: Calories: 240, Fat: 3g, Carbs: 40g, Protein: 12g, Sugar: 5g

---

TURKEY AND QUINOA STUFFED BELL PEPPERS

PREPARATION TIME: 20 min

COOKING TIME: 35 min

MODE OF COOKING: Baking

SERVINGS: 6

INGREDIENTS:

- 6 bell peppers, tops cut, seeds removed

- 1 lb ground turkey

- 1 cup cooked quinoa

- 1 Tbsp olive oil

- 1 onion, finely diced

- 2 cloves garlic, minced

- 1 cup spinach, chopped

- 1 tsp dried oregano

- 1 tsp dried basil

- Salt and pepper to taste

- 1 cup low-fat shredded cheese (optional)

DIRECTIONS:

1. Preheat oven to 375°F (190°C).

2. In a skillet, heat olive oil over medium heat. Add garlic and onion, sauté until translucent.

3. Add ground turkey, cook until browned.

4. Mix in cooked quinoa, spinach, oregano, basil, salt, and pepper. Cook for another 5 minutes.

5. Stuff the mixture into the hollowed bell peppers.

6. Place stuffed peppers in a baking dish and cover with aluminum foil.

7. Bake for 25 minutes. Remove foil, add cheese on top, and bake for another 10 minutes until cheese is melted and peppers are tender.

TIPS:

- For a spicy twist, add chopped jalapeños to the turkey mixture.

- Serve with a side of mixed greens for a balanced meal.

NUTRITIONAL VALUES: Calories: 290, Fat: 12g, Carbs: 22g, Protein: 27g, Sugar: 6g

OVEN-BAKED COD AND ASPARAGUS

PREPARATION TIME: 10 min

COOKING TIME: 20 min

MODE OF COOKING: Baking

SERVINGS: 4

INGREDIENTS:

- 4 cod fillets (each 6 oz)
- 1 lb asparagus, trimmed
- 2 Tbsp extra virgin olive oil
- 1 lemon, sliced
- Salt and black pepper to taste
- 1 tsp dried dill

DIRECTIONS:

1. Preheat oven to 400°F (204°C).
2. Place cod fillets and asparagus on a baking sheet.
3. Drizzle with olive oil, season with salt, pepper, and dill. Top with lemon slices.
4. Bake in the preheated oven for 20 minutes or until fish flakes easily with a fork.

TIPS:

- Serve with a side of quinoa or a fresh salad for a complete meal.
- Drizzle with freshly squeezed lemon juice just before serving for added zest.

NUTRITIONAL VALUES: Calories: 230, Fat: 8g, Carbs: 6g, Protein: 34g, Sugar: 2g

12.2 FREEZER-FRIENDLY MEALS FOR BUSY DAYS

QUINOA & CHICKPEA STUFFED BELL PEPPERS

PREPARATION TIME: 20 min

COOKING TIME: 30 min

MODE OF COOKING: Baking

SERVINGS: 4

INGREDIENTS:

- 4 large bell peppers, tops cut off and seeds removed
- 1 cup quinoa, cooked
- 1 can (15 oz) chickpeas, rinsed and drained
- 1 cup spinach, chopped
- 1 medium onion, diced
- 2 cloves garlic, minced
- 1 Tbsp extra virgin olive oil
- 1 tsp cumin
- 1/2 tsp paprika
- Salt and pepper to taste
- 1/4 cup fresh parsley, chopped

DIRECTIONS:

1. Preheat oven to 375°F (190°C).
2. In a skillet, heat olive oil over medium heat. Add onion and garlic, sauté until onion is translucent.
3. Add spinach, cooked quinoa, chickpeas, cumin, paprika, salt,

and pepper to the skillet. Cook for 5 min, stirring occasionally.

4. Stir in chopped parsley and remove from heat.

5. Spoon the mixture into each bell pepper and place them in a baking dish.

6. Cover with aluminum foil and bake in the preheated oven for about 25-30 min until the peppers are tender.

TIPS:

- Choose different colored bell peppers for a visually appealing dish.

- These stuffed peppers can be frozen and reheated for a quick meal.

NUTRITIONAL VALUES: Calories: 248, Fat: 6g, Carbs: 40g, Protein: 9g, Sugar: 7g

TURKEY & VEGETABLE MEATBALLS

PREPARATION TIME: 15 min
COOKING TIME: 20 min
MODE OF COOKING: Baking
SERVINGS: 4
INGREDIENTS:

- 1 lb ground turkey
- 1 cup cauliflower, finely grated
- 1 carrot, finely grated
- 1/2 cup onions, finely chopped
- 2 cloves garlic, minced
- 1 egg, beaten
- 1/2 cup whole-grain breadcrumbs
- 2 Tbsp parsley, chopped
- 1 tsp dried oregano
- Salt and pepper to taste
- 1 Tbsp extra virgin olive oil (for greasing)

DIRECTIONS:

1. Preheat oven to 400°F (204°C) and grease a baking sheet with olive oil.

2. In a large bowl, combine ground turkey, cauliflower, carrot, onion, garlic, egg, breadcrumbs, parsley, oregano, salt, and pepper.

3. Mix thoroughly until blended.

4. Form mixture into 1-inch balls and place them on the prepared baking sheet.

5. Bake in preheated oven for 20 min, or until meatballs are golden on the outside and no longer pink inside.

TIPS:

- Serve these with a dip made from non-fat Greek yogurt and dill for added flavor.

- Freeze the meatballs after baking and simply reheat for a quick protein-packed meal.

NUTRITIONAL VALUES: Calories: 190, Fat: 8g, Carbs: 12g, Protein: 20g, Sugar: 2g

---

SWEET POTATO AND BLACK BEAN BURRITOS

PREPARATION TIME: 15 min

COOKING TIME: 30 min

MODE OF COOKING: Baking

SERVINGS: 6 burritos

INGREDIENTS:

- 2 medium sweet potatoes, peeled and cubed
- 1 Tbsp olive oil
- 1 tsp cumin
- 1/2 tsp smoked paprika
- 1 can (15 oz) black beans, drained and rinsed
- 1 cup cooked brown rice
- 1/2 cup salsa
- 6 whole-grain tortillas
- 1/2 cup shredded cheddar cheese (optional)

PROCEDURE:

1. Preheat the oven to 400°F (200°C).
2. Toss the sweet potatoes with olive oil, cumin, smoked paprika, and a pinch of salt. Spread them on a baking sheet and roast for 25 minutes until tender.
3. In a large bowl, mix the roasted sweet potatoes, black beans, cooked brown rice, and salsa.
4. Lay out the tortillas and evenly distribute the filling onto each one. Sprinkle with cheese if desired.
5. Roll up the burritos tightly, tucking in the sides as you go.
6. Wrap each burrito individually in foil or plastic wrap for freezing.
7. To reheat, bake frozen burritos at 350°F (175°C) for 30-35 minutes, or microwave for 4-5 minutes until hot.

TIPS:

- Add fresh avocado or a spoonful of Greek yogurt when serving for extra creaminess.
- Freeze burritos for up to 3 months.

NUTRITIONAL VALUES: Calories: 330, Fat: 8g, Carbs: 50g, Protein: 12g, Sugar: 4g

---

CHICKEN AND BROCCOLI CASSEROLE

PREPARATION TIME: 20 min

COOKING TIME: 40 min

MODE OF COOKING: Baking

SERVINGS: 6

INGREDIENTS:

- 2 cups cooked chicken breast,

shredded

- 3 cups broccoli florets, steamed
- 1 cup cooked quinoa
- 1/2 cup non-fat Greek yogurt
- 1/2 cup low-fat shredded cheddar cheese
- 1/4 cup vegetable broth
- 1 tsp garlic powder
- Salt and pepper to taste

PROCEDURE:

1. Preheat the oven to 375°F (190°C).
2. In a large bowl, mix the shredded chicken, steamed broccoli, cooked quinoa, Greek yogurt, cheddar cheese, vegetable broth, garlic powder, salt, and pepper.
3. Pour the mixture into a greased baking dish and spread evenly.
4. Bake for 30-35 minutes, or until the casserole is bubbly and golden on top.
5. Let the casserole cool completely, then portion it into individual servings and freeze.
6. To reheat, bake at 350°F (175°C) for 25-30 minutes, or microwave until heated through.

TIPS:

- Add a sprinkle of breadcrumbs or crushed almonds on top for extra crunch.

- Freeze for up to 3 months in airtight containers.

NUTRITIONAL VALUES: Calories: 310, Fat: 10g, Carbs: 30g, Protein: 27g, Sugar: 2g

---

SALMON AND BROWN RICE FREEZER BOWLS

PREPARATION TIME: 15 min

COOKING TIME: 20 min

MODE OF COOKING: Baking and Assembling

SERVINGS: 4 bowls

INGREDIENTS:

- 4 salmon fillets (4 oz. each)
- 2 cups cooked brown rice
- 2 cups steamed broccoli florets
- 1 Tbsp olive oil
- 1 lemon, sliced
- Salt and pepper to taste
- 1 tsp garlic powder

PROCEDURE:

1. Preheat the oven to 375°F (190°C).
2. Rub the salmon fillets with olive oil, garlic powder, salt, and pepper. Place lemon slices on top of each fillet.
3. Bake the salmon for 18-20 minutes or until the fish is flaky.
4. While the salmon bakes, steam the broccoli and cook the brown

rice.

5. Once cooled, assemble the bowls: Add 1/2 cup brown rice, 1/2 cup steamed broccoli, and 1 salmon fillet to each container.

6. Cover and freeze the bowls. To reheat, bake at 350°F (175°C) for 25-30 minutes or microwave for 3-4 minutes.

TIPS:

- Squeeze extra lemon juice over the bowl before serving for a fresh burst of flavor.
- These bowls can be frozen for up to 2 months.

NUTRITIONAL VALUES: Calories: 350, Fat: 14g, Carbs: 30g, Protein: 28g, Sugar: 1g

---

VEGETARIAN LENTIL SHEPHERD'S PIE

PREPARATION TIME: 20 min

COOKING TIME: 45 min

MODE OF COOKING: Baking

SERVINGS: 6

INGREDIENTS:

- 1 cup dried lentils, rinsed
- 4 cups vegetable broth
- 2 cups mixed frozen vegetables (peas, carrots, corn)
- 2 large sweet potatoes, peeled and cubed
- 1/4 cup almond milk
- 1 Tbsp olive oil
- 1 tsp smoked paprika
- 1/2 tsp garlic powder
- Salt and pepper to taste

PROCEDURE:

1. Preheat the oven to 375°F (190°C).

2. In a large pot, boil the sweet potatoes for 15 minutes or until tender. Drain, mash with almond milk, olive oil, and salt, and set aside.

3. Meanwhile, cook the lentils in vegetable broth for 20 minutes or until tender.

4. In a large bowl, combine the cooked lentils with the mixed frozen vegetables, smoked paprika, garlic powder, salt, and pepper.

5. Spread the lentil mixture in a baking dish and top with the mashed sweet potatoes.

6. Bake for 25-30 minutes until the top is golden and bubbly.

7. Let cool completely before freezing. To reheat, bake at 350°F (175°C) for 30-35 minutes, or microwave until heated through.

TIPS:

- For a creamy topping, mix Greek

yogurt into the mashed sweet potatoes.

- Freeze in individual portions for quick and easy meals.

NUTRITIONAL VALUES: Calories: 320, Fat: 7g, Carbs: 55g, Protein: 12g, Sugar: 10g

12.3 READY-TO-GO LUNCHES AND DINNERS

MEDITERRANEAN TUNA AND QUINOA SALAD

PREPARATION TIME: 20 min

COOKING TIME: 15 min

MODE OF COOKING: Boiling

SERVINGS: 4

INGREDIENTS:

- 1 cup quinoa
- 2 cups water
- 1 can (15 oz.) tuna in water, drained
- 1 cucumber, diced
- 1 red bell pepper, diced
- 1/2 red onion, finely chopped
- 1/4 cup kalamata olives, pitted and sliced
- 1/4 cup feta cheese, crumbled
- 2 Tbsp extra virgin olive oil
- Juice of 1 lemon
- 1 tsp dried oregano
- Salt and pepper to taste

DIRECTIONS:

1. Rinse quinoa under cold running water.
2. In a medium saucepan, combine rinsed quinoa and 2 cups of water, bring to a boil, then cover and simmer for 15 min or until water is absorbed. Let it cool.
3. In a large mixing bowl, flake the tuna with a fork and add diced cucumber, red bell pepper, red onion, kalamata olives, and feta cheese.
4. Add cooled quinoa to the bowl.
5. In a small bowl, whisk together extra virgin olive oil, lemon juice, dried oregano, salt, and pepper.
6. Pour the dressing over the salad and toss to combine thoroughly.
7. Refrigerate until ready to serve or pack for lunch.

TIPS:

- For a zestier flavor, add a tablespoon of capers.
- This salad can be stored in the refrigerator for up to 3 days, making it perfect for batch cooking.

NUTRITIONAL VALUES: Calories: 330, Fat: 14g, Carbs: 33g, Protein: 20g, Sugar: 3g

CHICKEN AND VEGGIE STIR-FRY

PREPARATION TIME: 10 min

COOKING TIME: 15 min

MODE OF COOKING: Stir-frying

SERVINGS: 4

INGREDIENTS:

- 1 lb chicken breast, thinly sliced
- 2 Tbsp coconut oil
- 1 Tbsp garlic, minced
- 1 Tbsp ginger, minced
- 1 red bell pepper, julienned
- 1 broccoli head, cut into florets
- 2 carrots, sliced
- 1/2 cup soy sauce (low sodium)
- 1/4 cup chicken broth
- 1 tsp cornstarch
- 2 green onions, chopped
- Sesame seeds for garnish

DIRECTIONS:

1. Heat coconut oil in a large skillet over medium-high heat.
2. Add garlic and ginger, sauté for 1 min.
3. Increase heat to high, add chicken and stir-fry until browned and cooked through, about 5-7 min.
4. Add bell pepper, broccoli, and carrots to the skillet; stir-fry for another 5 min.
5. In a small bowl, whisk together soy sauce, chicken broth, and cornstarch; pour over the chicken and vegetables in the skillet.
6. Cook until the sauce has thickened and vegetables are tender but crisp, about 2-3 min.
7. Garnish with green onions and sesame seeds before serving.

TIPS:

- For added crunch, toss in a handful of unsalted cashews or almonds during the last 2 min of cooking.
- Serve over a bed of brown rice or quinoa for extra fiber.

NUTRITIONAL VALUES: Calories: 240, Fat: 9g, Carbs: 13g, Protein: 27g, Sugar: 5g

LENTIL AND SWEET POTATO BOWLS

PREPARATION TIME: 15 min

COOKING TIME: 30 min

MODE OF COOKING: Simmering and Roasting

SERVINGS: 4

INGREDIENTS:

- 1 cup dried green lentils, rinsed
- 2 medium sweet potatoes, peeled and cubed
- 2 Tbsp olive oil, divided
- 1 tsp cumin
- 1 tsp smoked paprika
- 4 cups spinach, wilted

- 1/4 cup tahini
- 2 Tbsp lemon juice
- 2 Tbsp water
- Salt and pepper to taste

PROCEDURE:

1. Preheat the oven to 400°F (200°C).
2. Toss the sweet potatoes with 1 Tbsp olive oil, cumin, smoked paprika, salt, and pepper. Roast for 25 minutes, turning halfway through.
3. In a saucepan, bring 3 cups of water to a boil and add the lentils. Simmer for 20-25 minutes, or until tender. Drain and set aside.
4. In a small bowl, whisk together the tahini, lemon juice, water, and salt to make a dressing.
5. Assemble the bowls with lentils, roasted sweet potatoes, wilted spinach, and drizzle with the tahini dressing.

TIPS:

- Add a sprinkle of sunflower seeds for extra crunch.
- These bowls store well in the fridge for up to 3 days.

NUTRITIONAL VALUES: Calories: 370, Fat: 12g, Carbs: 50g, Protein: 15g, Sugar: 7g

TOFU AND VEGETABLE STIR-FRY

PREPARATION TIME: 10 min

COOKING TIME: 15 min

MODE OF COOKING: Stir-frying

SERVINGS: 2

INGREDIENTS:

- 8 oz firm tofu, cubed
- 1 Tbsp coconut oil
- 1 red bell pepper, sliced
- 1 zucchini, sliced
- 1 cup broccoli florets
- 2 Tbsp low-sodium soy sauce
- 1 tsp sesame oil
- 1 tsp fresh ginger, grated
- 1 garlic clove, minced
- 2 tsp sesame seeds (optional)

PROCEDURE:

1. Heat the coconut oil in a large pan over medium heat. Add the tofu cubes and stir-fry for 5 minutes until golden.
2. Remove the tofu from the pan and set aside.
3. Add the bell pepper, zucchini, and broccoli to the pan, stir-frying for 4-5 minutes until tender.
4. Return the tofu to the pan and add the soy sauce, sesame oil, ginger, and garlic. Stir-fry for another 2 minutes.
5. Serve with a sprinkle of sesame seeds.

TIPS:

- Serve over cooked brown rice or quinoa for a heartier meal.
- Make it spicier with a dash of sriracha or chili flakes.

NUTRITIONAL VALUES: Calories: 300, Fat: 16g, Carbs: 22g, Protein: 18g, Sugar: 4g

---

SALMON AND FARRO SALAD

PREPARATION TIME: 10 min

COOKING TIME: 15 min

MODE OF COOKING: Grilling and Simmering

SERVINGS: 2

INGREDIENTS:

- 2 salmon fillets (4 oz each)
- 1/2 cup farro, cooked
- 2 cups arugula
- 1/2 cucumber, sliced
- 1/4 cup cherry tomatoes, halved
- 1 Tbsp olive oil
- 1 Tbsp lemon juice
- Salt and pepper to taste

PROCEDURE:

1. Grill the salmon fillets over medium heat for 4-5 minutes per side, until cooked through.
2. While the salmon is grilling, cook the farro according to package instructions.
3. In a large bowl, toss the cooked farro, arugula, cucumber, and cherry tomatoes with olive oil, lemon juice, salt, and pepper.
4. Serve the salad with the grilled salmon fillets on top.

TIPS:

- Make a double batch of farro to use in other meals throughout the week.
- This salad can be prepped ahead and stored in the fridge for 2-3 days.

NUTRITIONAL VALUES: Calories: 380, Fat: 18g, Carbs: 30g, Protein: 28g, Sugar: 3g

---

CHICKEN AND QUINOA MASON JAR SALADS

PREPARATION TIME: 10 min

COOKING TIME: 20 min

MODE OF COOKING: Assembling and Boiling

SERVINGS: 4 mason jars

INGREDIENTS:

- 2 chicken breasts, cooked and shredded
- 1 cup cooked quinoa
- 1/2 cup cherry tomatoes, halved
- 1/2 cucumber, diced
- 1/4 cup red onion, thinly sliced
- 1/4 cup feta cheese, crumbled (optional)

- 4 cups mixed greens (spinach, kale, arugula)
- 1/4 cup balsamic vinaigrette

PROCEDURE:

1. In four mason jars, layer the ingredients starting with the balsamic vinaigrette at the bottom.
2. Add the shredded chicken, quinoa, cherry tomatoes, cucumber, red onion, and feta cheese if using.
3. Top with the mixed greens.
4. Seal the mason jars tightly and refrigerate.
5. When ready to eat, shake the jar to mix the salad and enjoy.

TIPS:

- Swap chicken for tofu or tempeh for a vegetarian option.
- These mason jar salads will stay fresh in the fridge for up to 4 days.

NUTRITIONAL VALUES: Calories: 350, Fat: 12g, Carbs: 30g, Protein: 30g, Sugar: 4g

CHAPTER 13: REFRESHING DRINKS AND SMOOTHIES FOR WEIGHT LOSS

13.1 DETOX SMOOTHIES FOR CLEANSING AND ENERGY BOOSTING

GREEN DETOX ENERGIZER

PREPARATION TIME: 5 min

COOKING TIME: 0 min

MODE OF COOKING: Blending

SERVINGS: 2

INGREDIENTS:

• 1 cup fresh spinach leaves

• 1 medium green apple, cored and sliced

• 1/2 cucumber, sliced

• Juice of 1 lemon

• 1 Tbsp flaxseeds

• 1 tsp fresh ginger, grated

• 1 cup cold water

• Ice cubes (optional)

DIRECTIONS:

1. Combine spinach, green apple, cucumber, lemon juice, flaxseeds, and ginger in a blender.

2. Add cold water and blend until smooth.

3. Pour into glasses over ice cubes if preferred, and serve immediately.

TIPS:

• Ensure the apple and cucumber are organic to minimize pesticide exposure.

• Add a small handful of mint leaves for additional refreshing flavor.

NUTRITIONAL VALUES: Calories: 120, Fat: 1.5g, Carbs: 26g, Protein: 3g, Sugar: 15g

BERRY FLUSH SMOOTHIE

PREPARATION TIME: 5 min

COOKING TIME: 0 min

MODE OF COOKING: Blending

SERVINGS: 1

INGREDIENTS:

• 1 cup mixed berries (blueberries, strawberries, raspberries)

• 1/2 banana, sliced

• 1 Tbsp chia seeds

• 1 cup unsweetened almond milk

• 1/2 tsp vanilla extract

DIRECTIONS:

1. Add mixed berries, banana, chia

seeds, and almond milk to a blender.

2. Blend on high until smooth.

3. Add vanilla extract and pulse once more to mix.

4. Serve chilled.

TIPS:

• Use frozen berries to make the smoothie cold and thick without needing ice.

• If needed, sweeten with a teaspoon of honey or maple syrup.

NUTRITIONAL VALUES: Calories: 210, Fat: 4.5g, Carbs: 40g, Protein: 5g, Sugar: 20g

---

CITRUS-MINT DETOXIFIER

PREPARATION TIME: 7 min

COOKING TIME: 0 min

MODE OF COOKING: Blending

SERVINGS: 2

INGREDIENTS:

• 2 oranges, peeled and segmented

• 1/2 grapefruit, peeled and segmented

• 1 lime, juice only

• 1/4 cup fresh mint leaves

• 1 cup ice water

DIRECTIONS:

1. Combine orange segments, grapefruit segments, lime juice, and mint leaves in a blender.

2. Add ice water and blend until

smooth.

3. Strain the mixture through a fine sieve for a smoother texture if preferred.

4. Serve immediately for maximum freshness and potency.

TIPS:

• Drink in the morning on an empty stomach for best detox effects.

• Add a slice of peeled ginger for a spicy kick and additional metabolic benefits.

NUTRITIONAL VALUES: Calories: 120, Fat: 0.3g, Carbs: 28g, Protein: 2g, Sugar: 20g

---

TROPICAL TURMERIC CLEANSER

PREPARATION TIME: 5 min

COOKING TIME: 0 min

MODE OF COOKING: Blending

SERVINGS: 2

INGREDIENTS:

• 1 cup coconut water

• 1/2 cup pineapple chunks

• 1/2 mango, peeled and diced

• 1/2 tsp turmeric powder

• 1 Tbsp honey (optional)

DIRECTIONS:

1. Place coconut water, pineapple chunks, mango, and turmeric in a blender.

2. Blend until smooth.

3. Taste and add honey if additional

sweetness is desired.

4. Serve immediately to enjoy the full benefits of the nutrients.

TIPS:

• This smoothie can be enjoyed as a post-workout drink to aid muscle recovery and inflammation reduction.

• Ensure to mix well or blend again after adding honey to evenly sweeten the mixture.

NUTRITIONAL VALUES: Calories: 160, Fat: 0.5g, Carbs: 38g, Protein: 2g, Sugar: 32g

---

AVOCADO LIME REFRESHER

PREPARATION TIME: 5 min

COOKING TIME: 0 min

MODE OF COOKING: Blending

SERVINGS: 1

INGREDIENTS:

• 1 ripe avocado, peeled and pitted

• Juice of 2 limes

• 1 cup spinach

• 1/2 cup water

• Ice cubes

DIRECTIONS:

1. Place avocado, lime juice, spinach, and water in a blender.

2. Blend on high until smooth and creamy.

3. Add ice cubes and blend briefly to chill the smoothie.

4. Serve immediately for best taste and nutrient retention.

TIPS:

• This smoothie is particularly rich in healthy fats, making it an excellent choice for increasing satiety and supporting heart health.

• For a protein boost, add a scoop of plain, unsweetened protein powder.

NUTRITIONAL VALUES: Calories: 230, Fat: 15g, Carbs: 20g, Protein: 4g, Sugar: 2g

13.2 Low-Calorie Refreshing Beverages to Stay Hydrated

CUCUMBER MINT REFRESH

PREPARATION TIME: 10 min

COOKING TIME: 0 min

MODE OF COOKING: Mixing

SERVINGS: 2

INGREDIENTS:

- 1 large cucumber, peeled and sliced
- 10 fresh mint leaves
- 2 Tbsp fresh lime juice
- 1 tsp honey (optional)
- 4 cups cold water
- Ice cubes

DIRECTIONS:

1. Place cucumber slices and mint leaves in a large pitcher.
2. Add fresh lime juice and honey to the pitcher, if using.
3. Fill the pitcher with cold water and stir well to combine all ingredients.
4. Refrigerate for at least 30 minutes to allow the flavors to infuse.
5. Serve chilled, pouring into glasses over ice cubes.

TIPS:

- To enhance the flavor, let the mixture infuse overnight in the refrigerator.
- For a sparkling variant, replace half of the still water with sparkling water before serving.

NUTRITIONAL VALUES: Calories: 18, Fat: 0g, Carbs: 4g, Protein: 1g, Sugar: 2g

LEMON GINGER ZINGER

PREPARATION TIME: 10 min

COOKING TIME: 0 min

MODE OF COOKING: Mixing

SERVINGS: 2

INGREDIENTS:

- 4 cups of cold water
- 1 lemon, juiced
- 1-inch piece of ginger, grated
- 1 Tbsp honey
- Ice cubes

DIRECTIONS:

1. In a large pitcher, combine the fresh lemon juice and grated ginger.
2. Add honey to the mixture and stir until fully dissolved.
3. Pour cold water into the pitcher and mix thoroughly.
4. Allow the mixture to chill in the refrigerator for an hour.
5. Serve over ice in tall glasses.

TIPS:

- For a less pungent ginger taste, thinly slice the ginger instead of grating.

- Adding a pinch of cayenne can boost metabolism and add a spicy kick.

NUTRITIONAL VALUES: Calories: 25, Fat: 0g, Carbs: 6g, Protein: 0g, Sugar: 6g

BERRY CITRUS INFUSION

PREPARATION TIME: 5 min

COOKING TIME: 0 min

MODE OF COOKING: Infusing

SERVINGS: 2

INGREDIENTS:

- 1/2 cup mixed berries (blueberries, raspberries, strawberries)
- 1 orange, sliced
- 4 cups of cold water
- Ice cubes

DIRECTIONS:

1. Place the mixed berries and orange slices in a large pitcher.
2. Fill the pitcher with cold water.
3. Refrigerate for 2-3 hours to allow the fruits to infuse the water.
4. Serve the infused water in glasses filled with ice cubes.

TIPS:

- Mash berries slightly before adding to water for more pronounced flavor.

- For extra sweetness, add a small squirt of honey before refrigerating.

NUTRITIONAL VALUES: Calories: 30, Fat: 0g, Carbs: 8g, Protein: 0g, Sugar: 6g

GREEN TEA CITRUS COOLER

PREPARATION TIME: 5 min

COOKING TIME: 5 min

MODE OF COOKING: Brewing

SERVINGS: 2

INGREDIENTS:

- 2 green tea bags
- 4 cups of water
- 1 lemon, sliced
- 1 lime, sliced
- Ice cubes
- Fresh mint leaves (optional)

DIRECTIONS:

1. Boil water and pour over the green tea bags in a large pitcher.
2. Steep for 3-5 minutes then remove the tea bags.
3. Add sliced lemon and lime to the brewed tea.
4. Chill in the refrigerator until cold.
5. Serve over ice, garnished with fresh mint leaves, if desired.

TIPS:

- To prevent bitterness, do not over-steep the green tea.

- Add a few drops of honey if a sweeter drink is preferred.

NUTRITIONAL VALUES: Calories: 5, Fat: 0g, Carbs: 1g, Protein: 0g, Sugar: 0g

---

POMEGRANATE SPARKLING WATER

PREPARATION TIME: 3 min

COOKING TIME: 0 min

MODE OF COOKING: Mixing

SERVINGS: 2

INGREDIENTS:

- 1/2 cup pomegranate seeds
- 4 cups sparkling water
- Ice cubes
- 2 lime wedges for garnish

DIRECTIONS:

1. Divide the pomegranate seeds evenly into two large glasses.
2. Fill the glasses with ice cubes.
3. Pour sparkling water over the ice and pomegranate seeds.
4. Garnish each glass with a lime wedge.
5. Stir gently before serving to mix the flavors.

TIPS:

- Squeeze the lime wedge into the drink for an extra zing.
- For a cocktail version, a splash of vodka complements the pomegranate beautifully.

NUTRITIONAL VALUES: Calories: 35, Fat: 0g, Carbs: 9g, Protein: 0g, Sugar: 7g

13.3 PROTEIN SHAKES AND GREEN SMOOTHIES FOR POST-WORKOUT RECOVERY

LEAN GREEN RECOVERY SMOOTHIE

PREPARATION TIME: 5 min

COOKING TIME: 0 min

MODE OF COOKING: Blending

SERVINGS: 1

INGREDIENTS:

- 1 cup baby spinach
- 1/2 avocado
- 1/2 banana
- 1 scoop vanilla protein powder
- 1 Tbsp chia seeds
- 1 cup unsweetened almond milk
- 1/2 cup ice cubes

DIRECTIONS:

1. Place all ingredients in a high-speed blender.
2. Blend on high until smooth and creamy.

TIPS:

- Ensure the banana is frozen to

give the smoothie a creamier texture without needing ice.

- Add a tablespoon of almond butter for an extra dose of healthy fats and flavor.

NUTRITIONAL VALUES: Calories: 340, Fat: 15g, Carbs: 30g, Protein: 20g, Sugar: 12g

BERRY PROTEIN BLAST

PREPARATION TIME: 5 min

COOKING TIME: 0 min

MODE OF COOKING: Blending

SERVINGS: 1

INGREDIENTS:

- 1/2 cup frozen blueberries
- 1/2 cup frozen raspberries
- 1 scoop protein powder (whey or plant-based)
- 1 cup spinach
- 1 Tbsp flaxseeds
- 1 cup coconut water

DIRECTIONS:

1. Combine all ingredients in a blender.
2. Blend until smooth.

TIPS:

- Add a squeeze of lemon or lime for an extra tangy taste and vitamin C boost.
- Drink immediately after blending to maximize nutrient intake.

NUTRITIONAL VALUES: Calories: 295, Fat: 4g, Carbs: 35g, Protein: 27g, Sugar: 18g

CHOCOLATE ALMOND PROTEIN SHAKE

PREPARATION TIME: 5 min

COOKING TIME: 0 min

MODE OF COOKING: Blending

SERVINGS: 1

INGREDIENTS:

- 1 scoop chocolate protein powder
- 1 Tbsp almond butter
- 1 cup unsweetened almond milk
- 1 frozen banana
- 1/2 Tbsp cocoa powder
- 1/2 cup ice cubes

DIRECTIONS:

1. Place all ingredients into the blender.
2. Blend on high until smooth and frothy.

TIPS:

- For a thicker shake, add extra ice or use a frozen banana.
- Sprinkle a pinch of ground cinnamon for added flavor and health benefits.

NUTRITIONAL VALUES: Calories: 325, Fat: 12g, Carbs: 30g, Protein: 25g, Sugar: 15g

TROPICAL TURMERIC RECOVERY SMOOTHIE

PREPARATION TIME: 5 min

COOKING TIME: 0 min

MODE OF COOKING: Blending

SERVINGS: 1

INGREDIENTS:

- 1 cup frozen mango chunks
- 1/2 cup pineapple chunks
- 1 scoop vanilla protein powder
- 1 cup coconut water
- 1/2 tsp turmeric powder
- 1 Tbsp hemp seeds

DIRECTIONS:

1. Combine all ingredients in a blender.
2. Blend until smooth.

TIPS:

- Add a pinch of black pepper to enhance turmeric absorption.
- Garnish with a few mint leaves for a refreshing taste.

NUTRITIONAL VALUES: Calories: 310, Fat: 5g, Carbs: 45g, Protein: 20g, Sugar: 30g

AVOCADO LIME POST-WORKOUT SMOOTHIE

PREPARATION TIME: 5 min

COOKING TIME: 0 min

MODE OF COOKING: Blending

SERVINGS: 1

INGREDIENTS:

- 1/2 ripe avocado
- Juice of 1 lime
- 1 scoop protein powder (whey or plant-based)
- 1 Tbsp flaxseed oil
- 1 cup water
- 1/2 cup ice cubes

DIRECTIONS:

1. Scoop the avocado flesh into a blender.
2. Add lime juice, protein powder, flaxseed oil, water, and ice.
3. Blend until smooth.

TIPS:

- Adjust the consistency by adding more water if required.
- Serve chilled for a refreshing post-workout drink.

NUTRITIONAL VALUES: Calories: 330, Fat: 20g, Carbs: 18g, Protein: 20g, Sugar: 1g

THANK YOU FOR YOUR PURCHASE!

Dear Reader,

Thank you so much for purchasing my book! I truly hope it provides you with value and enjoyment. Your support is incredibly important to me.

If you could spare a few moments to leave a review, I would greatly appreciate it. Your insights help improve future works and guide others in their reading choices.

Also, as a special thank you, please scan the QR code below to receive your exclusive bonus content.

Once again, thank you for your support.

Warm regards,

Lenora Weatherford

Made in the USA
Las Vegas, NV
02 April 2025